Straws in the Wind

Straws in the Wind

Harry J. Boyle

PaperJacks

A division of General Publishing Co. Limited
Don Mills, Ontario

Published in PaperJacks 1973
Reprinted by arrangement with
Doubleday Canada Limited.

ISBN 0-7737-7039-9
Printed and bound in Canada

Table of Contents

"Though some make slight of Libels, yet you may see by them how the Wind sits: As take a Straw and throw it up into the Air, you shall see by that which way the Wind, which you shall not do by casting up a Stone. More solid Things do not shew the Complexion of the times so well, as Ballads and Libels."

JOHN SELDEN, "Table Talk" (1689)

To

The Editors of the *Montreal Star*

and

The Editors of *Weekend Magazine*

Foreword

This book is designed as an escape. Escape for the generation that's too old for pot and protest and too young for jogging or rocking chairs.

A great many of the items appeared in the *Montreal Star* and *Weekend Magazine*. I've arranged them into the semblance of a pattern for a year. The editors of both the *Montreal Star* and *Weekend Magazine* are concerned journalists. They know that the print media must reflect the trials and tribulations of Marshall McLuhan's technological age but feel we shouldn't lose sight of some of the unpleasant things which are still in existence.

Man, in particular North American man who crowds into high-rise apartments or exists on postage stamp lots in repetitive suburbs, protests about what is happening to his life. Scarcely removed from pioneer times, he blames "them" for changing values and environment without concern for the individual. He laments the inability to communicate with his children.

Each day he fights traffic, breathes polluted air and arrives at work filled with indignation. Then he proceeds to work diligently as a part of the complex which seems bent on making our natural environment uninhabitable. Questioned, he replies defensively that if he doesn't do it, someone else will.

This book is a look at some of the pleasant qualities which remain. Take a good look at them because they may not be around for too long. They say plastic domes will be the only protection for large cities and controlled hot house atmospheres. I wonder what the birds will think?

This collection is also Canadian. I am unashamedly Canadian. Not because I think there is an essential superiority in being a Canadian. I was born here and that's a good enough reason, and besides, through luck and circumstances we still have a chance, not only to make a good life and a just society, but also to demonstrate that in order to survive we must be active, not passive, members of the brotherhood of man.

1 *Sing No Laments for Canada*

We are essentially a private kind of people. This must be apparent by now, even to the noisy minority bent on trying to make us into pseudo-Americans. Our song of nationalism is a personal affair, but make no mistake, it is far from a lament!

The fact is, every Canadian has a song in his heart about the place of his upbringing. At times, he may have difficulties with the lyrics; but there's no doubt about the melody, because it concerns his birth and tender years, the most important happenings of his life. While the place of birth is accidental, and it is no more important to be born in Ontario than Tasmania or Nigeria, it's equally personal.

Each of us is the product of the heritage of our forefathers and the environment of youth. Transplanting at a truly susceptible time often brings stronger emotions and loyalties than inherited ones, in the way of the convert with the honed awareness of discovery. We are united, native and citizen by choice, in sharing an inner emotion, which at times can be almost sacramental.

I object to those who complain of a lack of a uniform libretto which theoretically must embrace all Canadians. That such a melange could be orchestrated is a fallacy. If it were, it would have the false notes of a television commercial. The true testimonial of a man for his country is personal and intimate, conserved for display on occasions such as Vimy or Dieppe.

My people came to this country to escape callousness, the indifference of absentee landlords and the Great Hunger. All around them were others barely removed from injustice, the lash, indentured poverty and the inquisitorial madness that replaced faith with zeal. They found freedom, and a land and a climate that gave bounty for hard work. Slightly in awe of the monumental space, they were mightily impressed by opportunity of free movement and thought.

Somehow, the founding Canadians were suspicious of patriotic jargon. They knew from experience how easy it is for the pat recitation to outshout the heart's quiet wish. They put their faith somewhat doggedly in institutions; some were patterned from habit, but many more were original and adapted to the circumstance. But always, in the face of stark and painful memories, they were designed to safeguard freedom and the privacy of the individual.

They learned to respect their surroundings, adapting to a climate staggering in its variation.

In a remarkably short time they conquered the heritage of fear, which is a natural endowment of oppression, and they prospered. The magnetism of the soil bound many of them until comparatively recently. To this day, there are traces of it in a surprising number of my generation.

The melody of my personal song is therefore based on the land, for my people are of the land. It doesn't matter where they hailed from, because the root causes of their escape were the same whether they were French, Scotch, Irish, Galician,

English, Russian, Ukrainian or what have you. The land they claimed and cleared was Canadian, and the Canadian soil was the backbone of the process of unifying them as Canadians. They cleared trees and planted their own solid feet in the soil and figuratively took root.

Forty years ago in a clapboard-sided log house on a side road in Western Ontario, the rawness of recent memories became the history of the moment. We were surrounded by pioneer artifacts. Certainly the black iron kettle had been moved from the kitchen to a pole in the barnyard for cooking feed. And the fireplace was boarded up and we had a deluxe kitchen range, the size of a modern diesel. But there was history all around. There was history in the imbedded and inked initials on the desk tops in the schoolhouse. It was frame, and it managed beautifully to be cold in winter and hot in summer, with two outdoor privies, prim and proper. The girls' faced east and the boys' west . . . . . and as for culture, we had calendar art! There was a strange assortment of calendar pictures, framed, such as the boy going fishing with the bait in a Magic Baking Powder tin, several gaudy ones of the Royal family, a badly darkened Angelus . . . . . and on the back wall, a very large and gory reminder of the '14-'18 War, donated by the I.O.D.E., and called "The Watch on the Rhine."

In this school I learned the British North America Act by rote and didn't understand it. It was another chore in the drab routine of education prescribed by a provincial department of education. I was dimly aware that the document made it possible for me to attend a Catholic separate school while my Protestant playmates attended a public school less than a mile away, administered by a different but equally penurious school board.

The ghosts of those days have remained with me ever since. Our history books ascribed all the good things to England, leaving most of our Canadian politicians anaemic. Even "John A." had a whitewash at the hands of our historians. It was all bland and tiring in the face of the fact that our firesides still rang with the stories of the locality. This was the Huron Tract, and we passed Gairbraid, the home of "Tiger" Dunlop, on our way to the county town of Goderich. This was exciting stuff and the final validity of the history books was destroyed by Irish grandparents with vivid memories of English injustice.

The environment of land affected many of us in our formative years. So I can remember the joy of reading in history that Samuel de Champlain was the first white man to recognize he truly loved Canada. It was apparent that his first significant act was not the building of a fortress at Quebec, but rather the extension of his patronage to Louis Hebert, the Paris apothecary who became the first Canadian settler. The Heberts farmed and raised children and this was the first full act of consecration, repeated over and over again ever since by every man and woman who blazed trees and cleared land for a homestead or a home site.

A countryman can truly not forget his land. He watches as the drying wind of spring sweeps gently in, shrinking the snow to hardy patches in fency corners and low marshlands. He tills it, fertilizes it, plants it and glories in the earth smell and the sounds of the spring season. He feels nature swell and pulse with life-giving sap as the trees mist and the fall seeding turns an almost unnatural green. Then, at night, he lingers on the back stoop, hesitating to leave his fields, caught in the eternal optimism of seed and growth.

Through the heat of summer and the golden burnished days of harvest, he is in a strange alliance, with weather as his fickle partner. Yet there is hope in the farmer whether he be a man who shares his harvest on sea and land, as in the Maritimes, or a specialist in the heartland of Canada, Ontario and Quebec. He has a bond with land and nature in the peach groves of Niagara, the cash crop area of Chatham or the sandy tobacco district at Delhi. The eternal optimist is the prairie wheat farmer. He has known, in the way of his fathers, the sudden vagaries of drought or wind or hail that can eliminate a whole season, going on with the hopeful phrase: "But next year will be the big one." It's the same on the cleared patch in a British Columbia valley, caught between the eternal brooding presence of the mountains.

The partnership of man and land is a very old one, dating from the time when he first discovered that by the effort of tillage and planting he could reap a harvest. For man, earth is a mother, often abused and neglected, sometimes shamefully exploited, and yet so willing in the face of renewed attention to forgive and to resume the maternal role of giving more than she receives.

Canada is a changing nation. The richness of her land is becoming apparent in other ways. The role of the farmer changes in importance; it is still vital, but now the contribution is greater from a smaller number of countrymen. A younger generation feels the exciting throb of progress and expanding cities and industrial flourishing, and writes its own song. The younger people can even be annoyed by the transplanted ones who resist transferring to the filing case life of high-rise developments. The promoter grits his teeth in frustration when he hears, "But, I like to have a little land. It's nice to have a place of your own. I don't know what I would do without a bit of land."

We are still close to the land. The city dweller may hear the sounds of spring if he strains and listens very carefully. He may even catch the siren call of migrating birds. If he strays into marshy lands still present in the suburbs, he may hear the peeping chorus of frogs, or bring home a bunch of pussy willows and wonder at the strange ache in his heart.

There were the sounds of the "'growing-up" years. On nights when our valley was held in the iron grasp of frost teeth, the trains moaned on the grade in agony. The express was a haughty creature that scudded through with derisive hoots. It ignored unimportant little places, because fancy goods and fancy people were destined for glittering places. The friendly "butter and egg" train that would stop for anyone always snorted saucily when he was penned on the siding to let his big and important brothers speed past.

The sound of the train whistle was an inspirational motif for many in the days when my family were awed by the space of the country. Yet, today, flight time rather than railroad miles is the reckoning factor of our land mass, and many a solitary worker is reassured of company by the drone of the jets. And my song must include the feeling of a first flight in a single-engine plane, giving a new perspective to the neat white houses and barns against the geometrical patterns of red soil and green fields of Prince Edward Island. Can any man forget the experience of flying into God's smoke wreathing the towering fanged peaks of the Rocky Mountains? No man can forget a black prairie night!

But a country is not all geography. It has a pulse of people, their voices and the words that live on. Canada is captured in the memory of Dr. E. A. Corbett triumphantly preaching the gospel of self-help to depression-riddled Westerners. I hear Dr. M. M. Coady drubbing hope into the consciousness of starving East Coast fishermen, his words and the quotations of his mentor, Father Jimmy Tompkins, punctuated by the waving of hands made enormous by hard, physical work. Can anyone doubt the quality of the heart's heritage in the patrician chiding benevolence of Georges Vanier?

They never doubted! They knew their warm hearts and the comfort of generous love. Nor did L. W. Brockington doubt when he plaited words into brilliant sonnets of praise for his adopted country. There was affection in Gladstone Murray and the men who pioneered a national broadcasting line to let Canadians hear each other and feel the strong tying bonds of human discourse throughout the length and breadth of the country.

I hear Canada in the broken accented words of a chuckling farmer who waited out the worst that drought, depression, drifting soil and Sow Thistle could do to him in Saskatchewan, as he surveyed his re-awakened land and said, "Hard times, eh? You should have been here. Why, times were so tough a jack rabbit would have to pack a lunch to cross a half-section."

I remember the retired Lunenburg man and his wife, pounding along in a converted bus on the Banff-Jasper highway.

"My God, these mountains are powerful. I lived by the sea and I fished the sea all my life, and I said to myself and the Missus, 'We're going to see the rest of the best country in the world before we die.' Well, we're doing it and it sure beats anything I ever dreamt about. But I'll go back to the sea and die there, happy."

Wasn't it Charles Dickens who said, "In the love of home the love of country has its rise."

I am unashamed of pride in the human foibles and monumental strengths of John A. Macdonald. There is a similar emotion for the traces of political rascality of a Joey Smallwood, and for the fierce determination of Dr. Gordon Shrum, who was told to build a university and brought into being British Columbia's breathtaking Simon Fraser. There's magic in the words and imagination of W. O. Mitchell and Earl Birney. Stephen Leacock might have made gentle fun of them, but he would have enjoyed Expo and Toronto's City Hall, and I don't think Sir Wilfrid Laurier would have been all that surprised at Place Ville Marie. And he would have been inordinately proud of Pierre Elliott Trudeau.

My appreciation of having been born in Canada is a deeply personal and moving thing. It is the pulse of my being, and somehow the deepest significance of locality often comes when I am away, and Canada comes into perspective in my consciousness. I remember once at night, when the Queen Mary had moved in mid-Atlantic from cold turbulence into the tropical atmosphere of the Gulf Stream. There was a great glitter of passengers luxuriating on the decks and someone asked the homeward-bound diplomat what he was thinking that kept him so quiet.

"They'll be cutting hay on the Tantramar Marsh now. I wish I was there. The Tantramar smells and feels like no place else on earth."

Identity?

Ask other nationalities. Like the Mexican who spoke to me, when I had just spent six weeks in perfect seventy degrees "escape from winter weather" in San Miguel de Allende.

"You're a Canadian?"

"Yes, how did you know?"

"Strange, but you can almost always tell. Canadians are somehow different from Americans or English. For one thing, I think you are more often lonely for your own country."

Tantramar Marsh, Toronto or Montreal, somehow we miss them and show it!

My song?

Personal as it may be, there is a wonderful satisfaction in knowing that it could be sung to perfection by Gilles Vigneault or Monique Leyrac. In fact, it would have to be sung by a fellow Canadian to get the proper expression and interpretation.

2   Cold Straws

JANUARY

Scientists are forever terrifying us about environment. We accept things too easily. Our cities are polluted and the air is often unfit to breathe. Our streets are dominated by vehicles, and we go on allowing them to encroach on the rights of pedestrians.

Relief is supposed to be coming with a new home environment. Cables and computers, picturephones and gadgets are planned to bring us all kinds of information and services so that we will be able to live and work in our automated cells. Robots will do household chores, but we secretly know that these monsters of gadgetry will ultimately take over in the manner of the motor car and reduce us to the status of being their servants.

If the prospect frightens you, strike a blow before it is too late and try using the natural environment before it all vanishes

9

under the hammer-headed march of so-called progress. There are still places free of highway builders and housing developers.

Tucked away in the folds of the hills, nestling by woods and swamps, or even plattered on flat, winter-stilled pasture lands, are the ponds of January. They are waiting for youngsters with new skates and oldsters adventurous enough to risk a few muscular aches and distortions.

Arenas and ice palaces are worthy, but poor substitutes for the open, glistening surface of a pond on a frosty January night. With a million stars studding the sky, a roaring bonfire and the shovelled snow on the edges like a giant safety ring, you will rediscover the virtues of fresh air, exercise and company. No electronic means of communication can bring the feel of a frosty nip on the cheeks, the bite of skates on crisp ice or the startling abstractions of lights and shadows on whirling skaters.

There are no computers on January ponds. If you know a scientist plotting the new environment, you owe it to mankind to take him along on a winter skating party!

WORDS OF WISDOM

The beginning year wouldn't be complete without an almanac. Even in an informational age, there is simply nothing to compare with the amazing matter contained in one of these booklets. Where else could a man like myself with an increasing forehead learn:

> "Whoever loses his hair should pound up peach kernels, mix them with vinegar, and put them on the bald pate."

That's only one example. In the whole history of jurisprudence there has probably never been legal advice to rival this for gaining a lawful suit:

> "If any one has to settle any just claim by way of a

law suit; let him take some of the largest kind of
sage and write the names of the 12 Apostles on the
leaves, and put them in his shoes before entering
the Courthouse, and he shall certainly gain the suit."

Marshall McLuhan says that we are addicted to antiques
because we are basically afraid of living in the present. The
almanac, while it is a relic of the past, is marked by at least
one modern attribute. It has been touched by inflation. In my
childhood there were at least two hanging on the pantry door,
provided free by drug companies, (which incidentally provided almost subliminal advertising throughout the collection
of information and "useful and entertaining material"). The
one hundred and forty-third edition, annual that is, of *Baer's
Agricultural Almanac* now costs fifty cents. The *World
Almanac* is selling at a dollar seventy-five.

I have long been a regular reader of Old Abe Sagendorph
and his *New England Farmer's Almanac*, but this year I was
lured by one edited by Gerald S. Lestz of John Baer's Sons,
Lancaster, Pennsylvania. Part of the reason was that I once
spent a delightful vacation among the Amish husbandmen of
the Pennsylvania countryside, where hex signs still adorn the
barns, and on the country sideroads there are more horse and
rigs than cars. The heading that it was a Bissextile Year had
a mark of nobility about it, which made me pass over one of
Hugh Hefner's catalogues of nubility in its favor.

Even at fifty cents it's a bargain. Where else could one find
a booklet containing "the rising, setting and eclipses of the sun
and moon; the phases and places of the moon; the aspects of
the planets, the rising, setting and southing of the most conspicuous planets and fixed stars; the time of high water; and
a variety of useful and entertaining matter including long-
range weather forecasts"?

Baer's Almanac has consolation for those unable to escape
our winter for southern exposure. It states that January, February and March will have normal temperatures, although

precipitation may be higher in February. Between January 12 and 15 it will be unsettled along the Great Lakes and into New England. During those three months the forecaster has been more than fair to us, but has put some nasty weather in the mountain and plains sections. That seems appropriate since obviously most customers are in the Great Lakes and New England area.

In 1867 they printed a statement and they are proud to repeat it. It went:

> "Men are like bugles; the more brass they contain
> the more noise they make, and the farther you can
> hear them. Ladies are like violets; the more modest
> and retiring they appear the better you like them."

Mr. Gerald S. Lestz is not a man to ignore the wisdom of the past. In 1596 a writer predicted that when a New Year's Day falls on a Monday, as it did in 1968, we would have "a winter somewhat uncomfortable; summer temperature; no plenty of fruit; many fansies and fables opened; agues shall raigne; kings and many others shall dye; marriages shall be in most places; and a common fall of gentlemen."

Baer's Almanac, unlike some of the ones of my memory, is not addicted to jokes. It prefers facts but some of these can be amusing. In Missouri, for instance, they found these listed causes of various deaths while searching very old records:

> "Went to bed feeling well, but woke up dead."
> "Died suddenly, nothing serious."
> "Don't know. Died without the aid of a physician."
> "Blow on the head with an ax. Contributory cause,
> another man's wife."
> "Had never been fatally ill before."

The first press for an almanac in North America was set up at Cambridge, Massachusetts, late in 1638. An Almanac for the Year 1639 was compiled by William Peirce. Considering this, I presume that we are safe in assuming that in spite of the electronic, informational age of McLuhan, almanacs will be around for a long time yet. As the editor says himself, "An hourglass never goes out of date; that's why we prefer manufacturing almanacs." With wisdom like that to puzzle over, who would be without an annual almanac?

WINTER ACTIVITY

City residents visiting the country may feel in the whitened world of winter something of emptiness. Yet for the person who wants to investigate there are all kinds of signs of life.

A fresh snowfall is an open invitation for country residents to leave marks as calling cards. Beneath the naked orchard trees there will be the coded signatures of the cottontail rabbits like exclamation points.

Mice leave lacy prints as evidence of their interest in granaries, feed boxes or even corn shocks standing neglected in a field. The raccoon, prowling on his nocturnal rounds, is betrayed by evidence which, at a casual glance, could have been imprinted in the snow by baby hands.

From house to barn there are circling lines showing sparks of adventure, as domestic pets like a cat or a dog have struck out on the new white canvas. Beside them you find where youngsters and even grownups have deliberately moved from a travelled path to make new trails.

The winter world, which has none of the buzz and hum of summer-busy creatures, is a quiet one. The countryman welcomes the marks because they provide constant reassurances that he is not alone in the hushed world around him.

EPIPHANY

Epiphany, from the Greek word Theophania, is interpreted as the showing forth of God. It is called Twelfth Day, happening that many days after Christmas as celebrated in the western world. It is also recognized as the Day of Kings.

There is a legend that the three Wise Men on their way to Bethlehem were asked by an elderly woman to wait for her until she was finished with her work, so that she might accompany them. It was the eve of Epiphany and she was loath to leave until her work was done, and the Magi were in a hurry. They bade her follow when she was ready, but she took time to make a present for the child of Bethlehem. She could not find them and has wandered ever since, carrying her gift. In Italy it is said that on this day called Befana she leaves presents, hoping to find the Christ child.

In the East, the feast is associated with the baptism of Christ in the Jordan, and from the lighted candles held at the ceremony comes the term "Feast of Lights." In certain places, the officiating Greek Orthodox priest throws a golden cross into the waters of a stream, which is recovered in the presence of the gathering by divers all seeking the honor of being first to salvage it.

In Canada it is a recognition of our pride as a people of great diversity that the Feast of Epiphany is celebrated by many groups, each in their own way. An Austrian family may still carry out the custom of taking hot coals and incense to each room of the house, and, in the country, to the barns. Following this, the Christmas tree is illuminated for the last time of the season, on the eve of Epiphany.

To all who share in the spirit of Epiphany, let us wish a sincere measure of joy, tendered with a full appreciation of their contributions to our nation as a whole.

ZERO WEATHER

The still grip of below zero weather is a reminder that we are still people of the North. The ice caps, in spite of dire predictions, remain in the Arctic regions and our locale hasn't been transformed into a sub-tropical one.

Forgotten now are the convertibles, open patios and swimming pools of summer. A Montreal man hears the chilling word "below," peers out at the hostile environment and adds another layer to his already bulky cocoon of clothes.

This phenomenon known as below zero is a sneaky adversary. It brings serious trouble to the unwary. Cars freeze up. Exposed hands, ears, in fact any part of the anatomy which is not protected, will be severely nipped.

Zero weather is something we can do very little about. Dreams of plastic bubbles to protect the city only remind us of the pollution which must first be removed. Temporary escape to a southern climate is a palliative depending on resources. We can, in effect, only bundle up and suffer, being consoled in a way by radio reports from Snag, Dawson Creek and Baffinland, where, as they say, "it really gets cold."

NOISE

Winter in the country has always been blessed by an absence of unpleasant noise. The sound of sleigh runners on hard-packed snow or the whooshing of skis on the slopes is harmonious. The bells of winter, especially in the time of horse-drawn conveyances, were pleasing.

Snow plows opened country roads for cars and trucks. It was a victory for locomotion, and a blow to winter serenity. But the countryman could always retreat on snowshoes or skis to a snow-locked retreat.

Now, invention of the motorized sled and toboggan means that the sanctuaries have been invaded. Practically no place is safe from the noisy worms of travel. Their passengers make littering a year-round phenomenon of North America.

Soon only the mountain tops will remain for solitude seekers, and even these remote eyries will yield to the blast of supersonic jets. We may yet become a continent of ear plug wearers. It will be our only defence against our own noisy inventions.

PIT APPLES

A younger generation may never have heard of them, but a countryman yearns at this time of year for the winter-ripe flavor of apples from an earthen storage pit. In the days before the freezing, flaking and deadening of natural flavor, farmers lined ground pits with straw and, in the days of fall, entrusted apples to them.

When supplies kept in normal storage began to deteriorate or dwindle or when the taste began to pale, it was time to open the winter pit. In bright, cold sunshine, the earth and straw would be peeled back until the spicy, earthy fragrance poured out. That first Russet, Baldwin or Northern Spy consumed on the spot would have in it a flavor compounded by the slow maturing in the earthy vault and would be reminiscent of winey, fall orchards.

A countryman closing the storage pit and wending his way through the cold, knifing air to the haven of a warm kitchen would certainly have entertained doubts about the apple in the tree part of the Garden of Eden story. On the other hand, he would be inclined to believe that Eve might easily have yielded to temptation if the apple had been proffered from a winter pit.

FROSTED WINDOWS

Can there be, in these days of abstraction, pop art, kinetic forms and all, any man-made creation to rival the natural forms of frost on a window pane? Here in delicate etching, with white on sparkling white, we see happenings which can never be derivative. Each is a new creation, vanishing under the tepid warmth of our northern January sun, leaving nothing more tangible than a memory.

To see a frosted window to perfection, stare through it from a night-chilled house when the Wolf Moon of January blazes full. You will see incomparable patterns of frond and fern, and mysterious conceptions touched by the icy light.

Exquisitely composed, they somehow suit and provoke contemplation of the stellar spaces. If a frosted window pane on a January night can provide such unexplainable phenomena, think of what man may yet behold as he probes new outer worlds and comes in contact with their unique natural orders.

3 *Oh February!*

FEBRUARY DISCONTENT

February is a month of discontent and vexation for the householder. There are all kinds of nuisances from icy, rutted roads to soft spells when motorists declare an open splashing season on pedestrians.

Enjoyment of the way the month is edging with longer days toward spring is marred by the certain knowledge of a blizzard. Also, how can you think of nature when a fuel dealer smugly announces an increase in price in mid-winter?

Overcoats and expensive outer wear, supposed to last for the season, mysteriously disintegrate around children. The car battery goes dead in a cold spell, only days after the warranty has expired. Families become conscious of the social disadvantages of being without a ski club membership. They promote ownership of a snowmobile.

All this can be tolerated. The supreme irritation is the endless recital by southward bound vacationers in office, restaurant and store about the sunny Utopia which awaits them. Now, in this chilly month of discontent we exist, aware that when they return their accounts will be reinforced with pictorial evidence of bright skies and warm beaches. It is almost too much to bear!

THE POND

An ordinary pond gives a dramatic insight into the ways of nature. To be an observer is to see at first hand the mystery of evolution.

For one thing a pond never dies. Even when it is covered with ice, the vegetation limp and dreary by its side, this laboratory of life is in a process of change. From frozen banks to mucky bottom, it is a seasonal dormitory for all manner of creatures from minute organisms to muskrats dozing in their lairs.

Long before the skin of ice is cracked by warmth and runoff water, the whole chain of life accelerates. Organisms speed up from bare existence to a pace where instinct restores the reproductive urge.

By the time the ice is gone and the trees have uncurled their clenched buds and leaf pods, birds and animals return to become predator and prey in the carefully planned ecology. It is structured and balanced, subject only to man's errant destructiveness.

In the new "rurbania" where man seeks to escape the demands of rural areas and the compartmentalized dreariness of suburbia, there is a place for ponds as reminders of nature's scheme of survival. Planners might consider them, since even a man-made excavation for a pond, given a reasonable amount of shrubbery, protection and a stocking with fish, soon develops a natural pattern.

A pond, requiring no attention except prevention of interference to remain pure for swimming, is a perfect lab for observation by children. It would seem to be preferable to a sterile, concrete and plastic swimming pool.

THE WOODPILE

The four men were New York executives but the guide said they were having more fun with the woodpile than they were in hunting. So much so that he began worrying about a sliced foot from a mishandled axe more than the possibility of their mistaking each other for an animal while brandishing a rifle.

"Those fellows lugged in wood until they had it piled everywhere and I had to tell them to stop. They split wood and at night there was a fire going in the fireplace that practically roasted us out," he related in astonishment. "They just couldn't get enough time for the woodpile. It seems strange fellows like that from a big city, messing around with wood. Splitting wood and bringing it in is just another chore for me. They thought it was fun!"

The four men at the deer camp were in their early fifties. One is president of a billion-dollar corporation. A second was his first vice-president. The other two are senior account executives for their advertising agency. Why would they be so fascinated with a woodpile?

In a way their story is typical. All were born in the northern states of Michigan and Minnesota, and three of them came from farms. One was from St. Ignace, a tourist town where Lake Michigan and Lake Huron meet. They are modern, progressive men but with a rural background.

"I remember as a boy having to fill up the woodbox when I got home from school," said the president. "I thought it was a dreadful job. My mother would nag me until finally my father came up from the barn and his orders were final. Then I did it. But somehow now I don't think of the work. There was the smell of beech and maple and sometimes birch stick and I remember the way they burned."

His vice-president recalled:

"One year we cut down an old orchard. The trees were all twisted and turned and my grandfather spent the whole summer and fall after they dried trying to split them. I remember when we put them in the woodshed, and when you went out there to get wood, they had a sort of spicy smell. When we burned that wood I tried to make the stove smoke a bit, just to get the tang of the apple wood smoke, but I had to be careful because my mother didn't want the wallpaper all blackened."

The advertising man wondered about his writers:

"I say to them, you've got to make people smell and feel things. Like I remember splitting wood in the summertime and the difference in fall when there was a touch of frost. It was tough in the summertime but you smelled the wood and the way the flies crawled all over it where the juice or sap dried. In the fall you hit a straight grained block and it just flew apart."

The man from St. Ignace remembered a fireplace in his grandfather's home:

"I used to sneak down after everybody else had gone to bed just to watch those coals. You talk about visions. There was just something wonderful in the way the coals built up and fell apart when a knot exploded. Somebody once described them as castles in dreams. I think that's about the way you would look at it. Sometimes my grandfather would come out in a long nightshirt with a stocking cap, and he'd sit down and smoke his pipe and say that old men don't need so much sleep. We would talk low so as not to disturb anyone and when the fire was getting grey with ashes he'd send me back to bed."

They sat, the four of them, and coaxed their memories with spiritual fortification and watched the fireplace and dreamed dreams so far away from Fifth Avenue as to be almost impossible to imagine. The war in Viet Nam caused them deep concern, but somehow not as much as the alienation of their own children.

"I sometimes think," said the president, "that my children should have been brought up with a woodpile to look after. Or maybe the discipline of the woodshed. They've missed something."

The vice-president confided, "My son has a place in Maine and I was horrified. There's all this wood around and do you know what? He burns oil. Says his time is too valuable to mess around with wood. I don't understand it."

It was getting late, and the man from St. Ignace yawned.

"Let's face it, you can't turn back. I bought a co-op apartment just off Park Avenue. Had a contractor put in a real fireplace and then I went looking for wood. You know something? I ended up paying fifty cents a stick at a delicatessen. Cost me over fifteen hundred dollars for the fireplace but I'm damned if I'm going to pay a half dollar for a measly stick of softwood."

The agency president said sadly, "I know a fancy-goods store where I can get you hardwood at a dollar a stick. Comes wrapped in gift paper. The way it is you can buy venison easier in New York than wood. Maybe we should take back wood in place of deer meat."

FEBRUARY CHANGE

February may be a tedious month for a city dweller tired of winter, but in the country it has indications of hope. The dawn is leisurely but earlier. Night departs like an unhurried guest taking the stars from sight, but the world holds their afterglow until the sun gleams cheerfully on ice and snow, water and window pane.

The countryman senses sap rising in the arterial system of the trees. It is linked with the fury of thaw-released flood waters on the earth's surface. The water of life in the trees rises, obedient to the control of nature. Flood waters rise and spill at their own whims, because of man's excesses and contradictions of the patterns of nature.

Even in February the observer senses preparation for spring.

Aspen, birch and poplar bark seems more highly colored. There is a supple evidence of life in the willow stems. A scampish blue jay sounds a trifle more impertinent. Perhaps he is only cheerful because he is optimistic about the subtle changes which are going on, in spite of the wintry impression of February.

COUNTRY MEMORIES

People with country loyalties do a lot of dreaming in these February days. They may even be found stopping in the suburbs at evening to listen for the sound of the nesting owls. A busy man will open his office window to savor the chirrupy chatter of the song sparrows. A woman will linger in a protected corner letting the sun warm her face.

On Saturdays they go searching at the market. Chances are they are prompted by memory and instinct. A jar of home-made maple syrup would send any one of them into ecstasy. They are subconsciously remembering the old fashioned "sap run."

Long before the present commercial tapping of maple trees, plastic piping and hygienic evaporators, this was the time of preparation on the farm. Spiles and augers were assembled. Buckets were counted and washed. The big kettles were moved back to their tripods beside the pile of firewood in the clearing.

This was the period of getting ready for the first harvest of the season, when the sweet sap was boiled during all-night vigils. Country people, now city people, are wrapped in the magical memory of the "sugaring off" time. That's why they move dreamily with their happy contemplation wrapped in sadness. It can never again be a reality, in spite of the intensity of the recollection.

THAW

Although we are inclined to feel that our winters have only a bitter monotony, reflection proves that they provide a variety of experiences. Nature has a habit of relenting after an extravagance of snow or an extended period of intense cold.

A countryman comes awake in the pre-dawn and senses that something has changed. The stillness has relaxed from the electric grasp of cold. It is simply softer! By morning there may again be a spasm of cold that makes the soft breath of the night crystallize in a grey and white world.

Within a matter of hours the wind gentles. The sun appears and the sky turns from grey to blue. Icicles on the sunny side of buildings make dripping splashes. By night, rain may come from some mysterious place. Again the cold comes back to give the world an ice palace appearance, and the morning sun shatters into prisms of strange and exotic light. But by noon the elements warm and go about shrinking the snow.

While released water forces new spillways and runoffs, and eases the coating over the faster waters, a pair of owls, fleeing from Arctic cold, appear to rest in swamp trees. Crows scold and a muskrat appears to survey the scene. He is canny, however, and not to be fooled, and goes back to his lair among the dormitories of earth where countless creatures sleep on, their natural clocks unaffected by temporary alarms or respites.

The thaw of mid-winter is a part of the master plan of the resting, living and dying in nature's design. For humans it is a relief, and, while there will be more periods of cold and harshness, it gives hope for the coming of spring and renewed vigor for the environmental tribulations ahead.

FULL SNOW MOON

Between the full Snow Moon of February and the end of March, the quickening sense of spring rouses even the city dweller. By night the world tightens with the lingering rage of winter, but the sun is our friend by day. We pin our hopes on that warming sun, and when Easter comes early by the calendar, anticipation broadens to hope for an early spring. There's justification in the dripping of the eaves, in the channeled run-offs of water and in snow wilting under its sooty coat of pollution evidence.

Spring comes with the surging power of released water,

symbolic of the fact that, even in the tightest-held time of winter, the sap has been readying for a life-giving surge through the arterial systems of plants and trees. There is the essence of life in the greening of buds and leaves and the chemistry of color in flowers and foliage.

Even in the seemingly sterile city there are places for the memory-haunted countryman to strengthen his faith with visual evidence. There's sticky resin on some bark and bulging buds on basswood and poplar in the park. The red dogwood is blushing.

The sparrows fuss like tiny gossips. The blue jays are winter-hoarse and inelegantly cheerful. Cardinals, nuthatches and chickadees have something to say. On soft days the smoke ground-hugs, and the distant noises of traffic and trains comes confusingly close. There's hope here as man's own arterial system surges in sympathy with nature. Even a blustering gale is only a temporary setback to the vibrant certainty of a spring awakening.

THE SNOW WE LOVE

Here we are in the middle of the long, dreary period between New Year's and Easter. And it's too long without a break.

What we need, urges Gordon Sinclair, probably the one working journalist in Canada wealthy enough to spend winter anywhere he wants, is a mid-winter holiday. Why not a frosty Mardi Gras honoring one of our great national assets, snow?

Snow?

Yes, snow.

Don't scream too loudly. It's a movement. Sinclair favors it. I like it.

This movement is based on the premise that native-born Canadians, in spite of their protests, are really geared to snow. After six weeks in the mountains of Mexico where the April and March temperatures never varied from 70 sunny degrees, my host grinned at my restlessness, "You miss the snow and the cold weather. All Canadians start by praising the warm weather and after a few weeks get jumpy. You have to have cold weather. It must be your metabolism."

It may be true. Canadians in the tropics at Christmas are a jumpy lot. They extol being away from slush, snow and cold, while trying to find trees that look like conventional Christmas ones. They gussy them up with everything from whipped soap suds to bleached cornflakes, trying to create the illusion of snow. It was a Canadian who hired a machine to dump a great pile of manufactured snow in a Florida shopping plaza. He wanted to show the local kids what they were missing by living in such a climate. He was lonesome!

Just imagine on this February day, how much snow there really must be from Cape Spear, Newfoundland, through the Laurentian Shield, the prairie north and the deep valleys of the mountain ranges of British Columbia.

Who can estimate? There have been some spectacular falls. During winter 1956-57, Kemano in B.C.'s Kildala Pass had 880 inches. On December 4, 1967, Fredericton, N.B. registered 30.5 inches. Don't let Vancouverites fool you about their misty paradise either! In December, 1964, they received 35.3 inches of snow!

We protest and yet when an open winter comes, everyone complains. People snuffle, wheeze and blame mysterious viruses on the "unseasonable" weather. Inner stubbornness won't let us admit we love snow.

One of the mysteries of modern living is how completely a heavy snowfall can paralyze a city. In Toronto, December 11 and 12, 1944, 22 inches fell on the city. It brought tragedy, causing the death of 14 persons, and everything came to a virtual standstill.

In the country such things are expected. Snow is a natural factor and you push it aside or go right over it. It covers the landscape and brings peace and a stilled sense of tranquility.

Yet many residents of Toronto still glory in reminiscing about the storm of '44.

"It was wonderful to step outside and not hear traffic. Neighbors, who had lived on the same street for years and never spoken to each other, got together and helped each other when the power went off, shared bread and milk and shovelled each other's driveways and stopped to talk. The talk was wonderful."

Anyone born in the country remembers the hushed feeling of waking in the before-dawn of a silent house. When you scraped the fronds of frost from the bedroom window, you found the world transformed by snow.

To be the first on the sleigh or toboggan to cascade down the powdered hillside was the thrill of a lifetime.

Now we may be coming to terms with snow. Call it what you will, but the mechanized bobsled is here to stay. Priced from $700 to approximately $1,000, Ontario expects thousands of them to be in operation this winter and has passed legislation forbidding them to operate on roads and highways.

Some parts of Canada already enjoy snow. February is the month when Quebec City holds its winter carnival. Vernon and Kimberley, B.C. have winter galas. At Barrie, Ontario, they have a purse of $5,000 for snowmobile races, while Penetanguishene features ice-boating. Waterloo University elects a Miss Canadian University Snow Queen. North Bay holds a fur carnival in March. Each year, the number of visitors increases the size of the Jasper and Banff galas. Who hasn't heard of Beaver Tail Soup, at The Pas Festival in Northern Manitoba, or the dog sled races in Ottawa?

To initiate a National Snow Festival, in conjunction with those already in operation, we need a symbol. Former Prime Minister and Mrs. Pearson were ski-dooers. But the answer may be in the two-seater hovercraft being built under patronage of the Department of Transport. A model to sell at $2,500 is displayed at the National Boat Show.

What a wonderful opportunity for Prime Minister Trudeau to honor snow and prove his adaptability to change! The television audience can watch as he declares the National Frost, Fun and Show holiday. Then, as Norman DePoe, describing the scene, is engulfed in a mass of frothing snow, the P.M. flits away from Parliament Hill to skim over the snow-clad Gatineau Hills.

A new, snowy era will begin for Canada! More important, we'll get a holiday break in this winter that seems to go on — and on — and on . . . . . . !

4 *March—Time of the Maple*

MARCH

Nature can be a tease and a hoyden in March. She takes advantage of our desires to be rid of winter to vent all kinds of capriciousness on the world.

You can never be certain of this month. A soft morning with a promise of spring can turn suddenly into a day frothing with snow. The morning walk in the sunshine has a habit of turning into a contest with a chilling wind that pokes out from behind buildings to snatch at you with chilly fingers.

The March world may close one day with the warm promise of growth, only to return cloaked in a white blanket. The wind is a bully. It shouts, bluffs and gusts with abandonment. It plays with clotheslines, harasses housewives and flicks icy darts at legs exposed so fully by mini-styles. Yet the wind of March melts the snow, coaxes the reluctant buds and dries the country hillsides.

28

March, for all its tantalizing, is a month of promise. We suffer the pranks because April holds out hope. It is only a few weeks away, and the soft and growing month will certainly be more than ample with her rewards for our patience.

TWILIGHT

Man has always been affected by twilight. Primitives know it as an interlude before shutting out the dark terrors of the night. Poets use the word to suggest peace and serenity. For children it is a period of frolicking before homework or bedtime.

Working man uses twilight for relaxation. Artists try to capture the subtleties of the fading illuminations. A retired man uses the term twilight for the years when he is released from the disciplines of work. Sailors, because the duration and color of twilight depend on the amount of condensed vapor in the air, use it to forecast weather. Bright, strange colors sharply outlining clouds indicate rain and wind. A wide, white sun in setting promises a storm. A setting in a faintly purple sky assures sailors of fine weather.

Now, as we leave the finality of day meeting night for the time of lengthening twilight, we accept it without too much examination, as the boon of an approaching spring.

TIME OF THE MAPLE

The thawing wind of the vernal equinox brings the sweet sap pulsing branchwards in the trunks of the hard maples. The farmer, responding in the way of his pioneer ancestors, taps the flow.

It's little wonder, because even the ancients didn't have an elixir to compare with maple syrup. When the clear sap, reduced by lengthy evaporation, turns from light amber to cherry brown, the product is surely man's reward for enduring a Northern winter.

The North American propensity for tampering in the name of hygiene or progress has standardized but not destroyed the flavor. Countrymen tasting it can even forget plastic collection tubes and shiny evaporators and remember the thrill of tapping with an auger, driving a spile and then sampling the sweet water" before the flow began "tink-a-tunking" in the bucket. Memory will help them relive feeling the sun in the sheltered bush where noisy congregations of crows cawed. They may hear the protesting groan of the bobsleigh on bare ground as they dumped the buckets in the collection barrel for the trip to the shanty.

They'll glory in their endurance of night vigils in stoking the fires while the steam whirled hellishly from the open bubbling kettles. They may even pine a bit for the somewhat unhygienic days when the presence of ash, coal or twig, only detected in the final straining, gave an added tang to the product of their labor — their own maple syrup.

"THE IRISH OF IT"

There were Irish overtones in my childhood, but it was apparent, even to me, that they were fading. Old men who remembered, or who fancied they remembered, the Old Country would chide younger people for apparent disregard of emotions and cherished prejudices. There was always the soft, lilting brogue that touched all of us, but even this came by degrees and there were some in the community who become only really Irish when they were, as the expression went, "Happy, mad, or under the influence."

It has always irritated me that, with so many generations on each side knowing only Canada as a birthplace, officialdom for so long would insist on my stating on an informational card that my ancestry was Irish. There was never any hesitation or emotion for the Irish tradition; it was just that the Canadian place of birth and surrounding stirred my blood a great deal more.

There was a certain amusing aspect of the whole thing. Once a venerable relative, who had never been in Ireland but talked as if his blood had been warmed by peat smoke, was aghast because a youngster thought he was referring to his rheumatism, when he mentioned the "thrubble."

Irritation with a younger generation wasn't confined to the Irish, however. Scottish communities, where elders kept their broad, thick accents and swarmed to Highland games to hear the pipes and the songs of Scotland, could be heard complaining of dwindling interest on the part of the younger people for sword dancing and tossing the caber. It is said that the sight of a granddaughter, dressed in a Highland costume, doing the Charleston, hastened the death of a MacNeil who lived near Lucknow and was even opposed to organ music in the local kirk.

The Irish heritage touched me as a child in many ways. There were times at home, with only the firelight flickering from an open grate in the stove or from cracks in the top and casting dancing ribbons on the walls, when the older people would start talking in what seemed to be almost a foreign language. It sorted out and there were stories of banshees wailing, proclaiming the death of a near one before the news could be heard.

In college, I came in contact with a teacher with an Irish name and fervently nationalistic streak. He singled out students with Irish names for his particular attention, much to our chagrin, because he considered it almost heresy that we were so lacking in knowledge of Ireland.

Youth can stand almost anything but ridicule, and I was the butt of his when he said once with extravagant sarcasm, "We will now have the privilege of a man called Boyle explaining the theory of Boyle's Law, promulgated by Robert Boyle, son of Richard, the great Earl of Cork." I was sorely lacking in knowledge, and the experience reduced me to a quivering rage.

It also left me ripe for cultivation by another student, who provided my first experience with a breed which in grown-up life is known as "confidence" men.

"I can give you the whole story of your family in Ireland,"

he said. "Genealogy is my pa's speciality back home in Dublin. I'll get you all the facts and you can put that jackanapes in his place."

Money was scarce, but I parted with ten dollars to learn that the family motto was "Dominus Providebit," which translated into "The Lord Will Provide." In flowery language, the family was traced back to Conal Gulban, son of the King of Ireland in AD 379.

Fate took the instructor on to a college in the United States and I was never able to use the information in a classroom. The typed notes, about two paragraphs on a single sheet of paper, which seemed skimpy for ten dollars, did however provide some titillation with my family, although I never told them the cost.

Years later in Dublin, with time to spend, I chanced to show it to an acquaintance with a hazy idea of discovering ancestry. He took a pull of his pipe and a sip of his brew and looked at me quizzically for some time, as if trying to determine just what to say.

"I wouldn't be showing that too much," he said quietly. "For some time, a number of years ago, there were cards in tea packages with these ancestry lines and that one looks mighty like one of them. In fact, it's word for word."

Then he added gently: "It was a kind of a pull put out by the tea packagers to sell over here. You see, the tea was put up in England."

SPRING RAIN

Spring rain is a benediction of Nature on winter-tired cities. In the country, it is the sign of a re-awakening, but in the cluttered urban areas it is also a soothing and cleansing agent reaching beyond the physical and applying psychological balm to winter-scarred souls.

The arrows of the spring rain have gentle tips that bear no malice, misting on faces and bending to bead on clothing like miniature jewels. The rain spreads pools and tiny ponds to mirror tomorrow's anticipated blue sky and warming sun.

Fingers of the sky water coax forgotten hyacinths, tulips and golden daffodils to splotch random colors on drab, earthy surroundings. Rain makes men, long removed from agrarian backgrounds, ignore the winter debris on postage stamp lots and envision glorious profusions of vegetables, flowers and green lawn.

Something about the rain makes shipping clerks and corporation presidents skip lunch and meet on an equal basis in hardware stores. Here, with glistening eyes, they let grass seed trickle sensuously through their fingers, heft hoes, spades and rakes and speak knowingly of clover, fescue, perennial rye and Kentucky blue grass. They are united in a solemn vengeance on the common enemy, crabgrass.

They leave somewhat intoxicated with the mingled aromas of enamel, metal, grass seed, machine oil and weed killers. While the rain mists on the imprisoning office windows, they dream an afternoon away, and then, hurrying home with their purchases, are anxious to begin optimistic new gardening efforts.

A wise wife resists the temptation of pointing out last year's purchases, still intact in the garage or basement. Every man is entitled to dream a little when held in the grip of spring rain. The new hoe, grass seed and fertilizer are merely an offering to Iris, goddess of the rain, who displays her most alluring aspects in the spring.

SQUIRRELS

A pair of courting squirrels in spring must be the most agile and demonstrative of all the animals yielding to the housekeeping urge.

They flit from limb to limb and take breathtaking leaps, while the female maintains the fiction that she is trying to escape. When the ritual is over and formal arrangements are set up, the male is inclined to go back to his gad-about habits, but the female takes her role seriously. She guards her helpless offspring and yields to wifely traits such as rearranging or even changing nests.

Baby squirrels must be taught to climb, and instincts for self-preservation have to be honed to perfection. There are tumbles galore in the trial runs and plenty of fun for human spectators. In late summer or early fall nature asserts a new sense. The companionate frolicking gives way to a parting of company, sometimes in a noisy squabble.

Thus begins the annual stocking of the winter larders. With the help of the protruding eyes that give them sweeping vision in all directions, they set out to make provision for the leaner days of winter. They can become a nuisance if they make a house attic into a hoarding, and will show amazing resistance to human discouragement.

In an age when most creatures find it increasingly difficult to survive in the face of man's development of suburban living, the squirrel is tough and adaptable. The red, black, grey or flying squirrel is a saucily independent fellow-inhabitant of the earth, and we are fortunate to have him remain as a colorful neighbor.

SPRING RITES

Every man is aware of the trying times when the woman of the house embarks on the rites of spring cleaning. Some feel it is an inherited instinct going back to the cave woman. Primitive woman must have pulled aside the fur curtain at the cave mouth, felt the warming urge of the sun and the stirring sense of nature, and responded instinctively by launching a campaign of "redding up."

In the way his hide-garbed ancestor resisted, so must modern man protest. It is presumed that there was an objection to the disposal of an interesting mastodon bone, for the same hazy reasons today's head of the household guards old magazines, a leaking hose or a broken transistor radio.

"It's perfectly all right. At least it will be when I do something with it."

It's painful for a man to see a woman plunder attic, basement, den or garage. He hovers like a helpless bird fluttering at a predator. When other duties call his wife, you'll see him smuggling away a battered fishing hat, the rubber boots that have needed fixing for years and the old phonograph recordings he imagines may be of value.

Triumphantly he hides his rescued trove, braving his wife's wrath with the comforting thought she is suffering a form of "spring madness" which has distorted her sense of values. He is secure when he finds her finally staring dreamily at objects of her own concern or replacing frocks in the closet with the assertion that their style is almost bound to return.

Just the same, it is a trying time for a man with his sensitive appreciation and sentimentality for broken but valuable relics of the past!

5 *April*

A CITY IN LOVE

Great cities respond to spring like charming women re-awakened to love after a winter of neglect. They lavish affection, hoping to insure against the return of the chilling time.

A city deserving of love in return is a romantic place. It splashes color like a coquette, misting trees with green and frothing blossoms on bushes that remain undistinguished for the rest of the year. It cajoles the colorful ranks of tulips to come to attention, like miniature guards of honor, along park avenues and paths. The purple gauzery of lilac seduces the pollen laden honey bees, while the chattering squirrels gossip and take up their new domestic cycle.

The open arms of a spring-happy city strains the soft wind to a caress. It has vacant lots to provide high adventure for small boys, ponds and small lakes for migratory fowl, and bench-dotted parks for those who only observe. It abets the cause of dream-filled lovers with quiet corners and secluded nooks.

Safe from the roar of traffic there are retreats for fond mothers to gossip and watch toddlers struggle for balance. Impartially, it also provides spots where girls may watch and wait, hoping that a curious glance will convey a signal without being misinterpreted as boldly provocative.

The crack of bat on ball and the joyous sound of youth must resound on the green flats or in the safety of one-way streets. Man must also have grassy slopes where he can sprawl in the warmth of the sun, renewing his strength and sensuous affinity for earth, while sensing the pulse of growth.

By night there is mystery in the great city. A man yearns at the sight of the riding lights of sea vessels sighing at anchorage. Happy laughter steals down in a disembodied way from the high slopes and the basket porches of shafted buildings. Late walkers saunter as if reluctant to go in out of the velvet air. A car whispers along a silent street, the shush-whapping swallowed up in the distance.

The lights wink out, and a great city is content with the new season and with a warm, pulsing heart that has rediscovered the joy of loving and being loved.

WAITING GAME

Winter is an ungraceful loser. Like a punch-drunk boxer it flails futilely at contending spring with icy blasts that cause the inconvenience of a delayed decision. It refuses to accept the calendar's technical knockout.

Bowing to daytime sun and the drying wind, it forms conspiratorial cabals with dissident breezes lurking in dark streets and alleys. They nip and flick icily at unwary pedestrians, leaving "goose pimples" on bared arms and legs, as reminders that the new season is not yet a total victor.

Winter enlists mercenary Arctic forces to rage in the upper reaches against the warming southern currents summoned by spring. Apart from tormenting forecasters, double-crossing the natural instincts of migrating birds and mystifying the optimism of early gardeners, it avails only temporary setbacks.

The wind has meagre triumphs at night in the face of an uninvolved moon. It mischievously torments buds and eager blossoms and skins open water with ice film. It invokes ephemeral blizzards, causing motorists to have morning apprehensions, but the triumph is meagre, and the snow vanishes in the face of the smiling sun.

Winter is playing a waiting game but a losing one. The owl knows this because his age-old instincts are responsive to light and the lengthening days; and he also knows that his mate warming a crude nest in the frozen marshland signifies the true defeat of our tenacious Northern winter.

THE WATCHERS

A country expression says, "a wise man knows when the sun is on the right side of the fence." Similarly, old men who have triumphed over the pain of a city winter and the hazards of age know when the sun is on the right park bench. Here, nestling in the lee of a monument or a building, protected from the lingering spice of cold in the wind, they come to appreciate spring.

Winter-interrupted conversations and endless reminiscences are resumed. They air grievances and resentments against family, landlords or institutions, made poignant by winter confinement, and they feel better in the sharing.

Pipes wheeze and tobacco smoke wreaths their heads. They are genuinely delighted as the group of cronies straggle back, and the numbers are tallied, for they are truly survivors of the winter campaign. They don't dwell on the gaps, because battle experience has taught these old soldiers of life that grieving against fate is a form of total futility.

There is a ritual in deploring prices, taxes, politicians and dangerous traffic. The daily round of crisis in careers, in which they once participated so fully, is now an object of curiosity to be observed from the sidelines. They may even wonder a trifle sadly why concern was allowed so often to overshadow satisfaction in living.

Now they eagerly hoard the feeling of a sun-touched breeze, the glory of awakened tulips and daffodils, the return to spring domesticity of favorite park robins or the slowly misting green of the trees.

They chat, smoke and glory in treasured life. Habit may bring critical words for modern female dress and deportment. Yet, the eyes deny the scorn and reflect only the inner satisfaction of still being able to appreciate the twinkling of shapely legs revealed so fully by abbreviated fashions.

DREAMING IN THE SPRING

"God made the country," wrote William Cowper, "and man made the city." This observation seems to have a great force with the city man in Spring when he crowds suburban real estate offices or drives into the country, wistfully looking for a "place." He is looking for a dream, a part of the pattern of the expatriate agrarian or the son of rural parents who refuses to come to grips with urban living and compromises with Utopian myths.

The pieties about small town and rural living, the wistful dreams of independence and the desire to escape from what they consider to be the ugliness of the city, can be soul destroying. Most of those who urgently desire a sylvan retreat will never be able to afford one. They move through life missing the advantages of the city and substituting unrewarding daydreams. Those who manage to move find more than they bargained for, caught in a situation which can be hostile.

Living in the country requires an adjustment and a new arrangement of living. The countryman has the discipline of work and the regimen of habit. Machinery and technology removed a good deal of the former tyranny of work, which at times was slavish. In addition, the satisfied countryman has come to an arrangement with his environment, because he knows that in the final analysis Nature is a force to be co-operated with, and never resisted.

The transplanted man will glory at first in freedom from the irritants of smog, pollution, congestion, traffic and noise. Noise can take many forms: against the quieter background he will find the sound of the trilling rooster glorying in the risen sun to be disturbing after the first flush of enthusiasm. Like the visitor to the jungle, unaccustomed to nature, he will find that new sounds have a habit of dwarfing familiar ones. Farmers work heavy machinery, and in busy seasons they ignore the niceties of union arrangements and may go by the twenty-four hour cycle.

He will find that new tensions will replace those he shed at the city limits. They build during power failures when local inhabitants accept the break cheerfully and workers take an inordinate amount of time to repair the convenience. The hair on his neck stiffens as he tries to carefully code a business message on a party line prickling with interested eaves-droppers. Tradesmen supplying services of all kinds, from the man who fixes the septic tank, to the leaky roof mender, who would be considered hopelessly inefficient in the city if he did not respond in a matter of hours, may delay for days in the country.

A woman who found recreation and relief from housework in simply going downtown on the bus or subway to window-shop or browse in strange stores will find it vastly different in her new community. Local stores exist as a service, and what is not available will be ordered. She comes to understand the preoccupation of local residents with the mail order catalogue.

The new settler who yearns for the thrill of participating in democracy on the local level may have a shock in store. Com-munity interest may be misinterpreted as meddling in the face of administrations gripped by entrenched hierarchies. He may discover his own casual religious interest to be positively revolutionary in the face of doctrines preached with overtones more fundamental than ecumenical.

Privacy, which he bemoaned as isolation in the city, may have a new value. It amuses him at first to find so much interest in all his activities. He responds to questions about his work, plans and movements. Then he feels secret eyes watching all the time and, growing uncommunicative, finds an estrangement with people with whom he ardently wants to share a fellowship of interest. But the interests which he has acquired in his more sophisticated environment are practically unknown, and he has to either settle for wisps of community gossip or pursue his solitary way.

He still has the expense of lawn and garden and he yearns for the satisfaction of waistline reduction and table serving. He will learn the wisdom of Oren Arnold when he wrote: "Those manuals of make believe, the seed catalogues, have one weakness; they don't tell me how to sustain my April gardening enthusiasm through the heat of July." A session of "growing his own" will make many a would-be agriculturalist realize the harassment which can be given by a bountiful nature in the way of bugs, disease and drought. The fruit and vegetable displays of the supermarket or country market will afterwards stand as monuments to the ability of the farmer to make nature co-operate.

Reluctantly, many people will come to see that man has been making cities through the ages. Mayans, Romans and Greeks made cities, and they lived in them. We introduced the industrial element, the tyranny of private mechanized travel and a host of other discouragements to enjoyment, but cities will go on and they must be tamed to give man a satisfactory environment. Retreat will never accomplish this, nor will a sulky withdrawal from responsibility and a failure to appreciate what the modern city does have by way of advantages.

It's too bad so many "rurbanites" have to learn that Utopia is not automatically situated in the country. Indeed, if they adjust to their own surroundings, they may hear what Jimmy Durante calls the joy of there always being a band on the next street.

PUSSY WILLOWS

It is still possible for a boy to reach the edge of the city and find adventure in marshy spots where water runs free and the willows grow in profusion. It's a dwindling luxury as the suburbs engulf the surrounding areas, but the sight of a dishevelled boy bearing a bunch of pussy willows indicates that it hasn't completely vanished.

Salix, the willow, has over seventy-odd varieties in North America. Most of them are hardy enough for our Canadian weather and topography. For instance, the majestic Black Willow (Salix Nigra) ranges from the Maritimes to Ontario, and the graceful Peachleaf (Salix Amygdaloides) grows from Ontario to British Columbia.

The willow family (Salicaceae) is a friend to man, yielding salicyn from its inner bark, giving countless people employment in extolling the virtues of the derivative aspirin as a headache remedy. Girls, especially those who yearn to grace the pages of fashion magazines, respond to the descriptive word "willowy" with appreciation. The willow pattern is almost a classic in dishware from English potteries.

Few people fail to recognize the drooping, yellow branches in the early spring of the weeping willow. A species of the family (called Babylonica) is said to be a sign of unlucky love and sorrow, dating back to the legend that Christ spent his last night in the shadow of a willow in Gethsemane.

Yet it is the twigs of willow bearing the familiar catkins that strike the most responsive note. A man confronted with them on a vendor's cart can be forgiven for dreaming a little about his youth. There was nothing in the summer like a skinny dip in a pool made by a river bend sheltered by clustering willows. The pussy willows of spring evoke memories of the sounds of rushing water, frogs in full chorus and scolding crows.

A mother receiving a clutch of the slender limbs with the tiny, silken catkins like timid miniatures hanging on for dear life may remember they are symbols of a sun-warmed era when everyone was inclined to a languid disregard for the tyranny of time.

Such a peace offering should erase the anxiety of her vigil and the annoyance of damaged clothes, and help her glory fully in the majestic devotion of a small boy.

EASTER HATS

An Easter hat is a bright badge of courage. It signifies the eternal optimism of woman against the drabness and soul-withering quality of a lingering winter.

It must be a tiara of color, bold in regal glory, perhaps flippant in texture, intriguing in unconventional design and always capable of attracting attention. Even the most retiring wearer will anticipate the gauntlet of curiosity which may register anything from amazement to amusement.

Carefully treasured in tissue, the perfect headpiece glows away like a warm pulse on the wardrobe shelf. When children strain tolerance, the unattended TV irritates, transistors screech, the telephone pesters and deliverymen are tardy, the mere thought of its radiance can be a consolation.

How many wives at the close of a wearying day, when husbands contribute only monosyllabic signals in place of conversation, may find solace with The Hat. For pleasurable moments they enjoy the vicarious thrills of heirs apparent privately trying on crowns and substituting dreams for realities.

Come rain, shine or chilly bluster, an Easter Sunday is the beneficiary of the assorted display. Like radiant jewels the bonnets, hats, chapeaux or call them what you will, brighten the hushed and dusky places of twentieth century worship. If devotion is rivalled by comparative speculations, it is no heresy, for women are merely following the pattern of nature with new finery to honor the arrival of Spring, the season of hope.

THE LURE OF WATER

The shortest way home, according to a boy in spring, is by way of the maximum number of mud puddles. Some primal instinct links the youngster with water, but does not increase his regard for it as a cleansing agent.

Just as a country boy investigates creeks and ditches, so also does a city boy seek out water in pot holes, gullies and truck-rutted channels on construction sites. A shingle or board with a lollipop stick and paper as mast and sail becomes a stately schooner, barque or brigantine in his mind's eye. He is also prone to a great deal of engineering effort in creating diversions.

Molded mud shaped by foot, hand and metal scrap can become a transportation rival to the seaway. Here a great dam comes into being that overshadows the mighty Manicouagan. Finally there is the genuine delight of simply splashing and being splashed by the sluicing waves of muddy water.

The moment of reckoning comes when a scolding mother divests the culprit of damp clothing and muddy boots. The action is usually accompanied by dire predictions of chill, cold, and pneumonia. When the oral chastisement fails to produce the proper effect, there is an appeal for paternal intervention.

The boy is safe. The father shares the secret of the lure of water in the spring. He will feverishly find a way of delaying punishment until memory dims the gravity of the act.

A man has compassion about these things. He understands, because after all who drove down to the harbor to watch the ships loading at noon? Who still feels the caress of the seductive "sea wind" on his cheeks? Who was interrupted by the return of the boy, while dreaming of may-flies and sun-dappled pools with lurking trout?

A man remembers on a day like this. He is carried back to sense the pulse of flood-swollen creeks and rivers of his country boyhood. He wishes, a trifle sadly, that he could share it all with the boy who has resorted to mud puddles, but under the vigilance of an aroused wife and mother, he dare not recall the raft and the urging which sent him scurrying to sea on a day when the lure of water and the spring proved to be a fascination.

MUD

Spring is a time to be reminded that some aspects of progress are beneficial. Modern, paved roads are utilitarian and often unfair to aesthetics; yet they do control the mud of spring and fall.

A few years ago, April and November were months of horror for travellers in the country. Viscous, oozing mud brought vehicles to a halt.

The dirty, brown stuff clutched taffy-like at wheels until they slowed down to a mired stop. A trip on foot to enlist the services of a farmer with a husky team of horses for salvage work was an ordeal. There was ignominy in admitting defeat. There was sheer torture in the effort of trying to negotiate secure footing on stones or grassy patches, which were miniscule islands in the sea of mud in all country roads and laneways.

Travellers suspected chicanery. They said farmers kept potholes watered to a treacherous consistency, then brazenly stood by with horses hitched for emergencies at set fees.

Today, except in remote places, mud has been conquered. April is one time when we are moved to forgive the planners for their ruthlessness in pushing roads and highways across the land, because they have given us mastery over mud.

APRIL POWER

Nature is firmly in control in April. Man is only a bystander as his natural environment undergoes a re-awakening. He can only marvel at the power.

Warm days, cool nights, a harsh day or a freakish, torrid day are all part of a pattern that pushes the growing process along. From deep roots, the sap pulses upward in trunks, limbs and stems to nudge buds and blooms into full life. The grass greens imperceptibly until we are surrounded by bright lawns and fields.

Water surges down from the hidden recesses of the forests and hills. Tiny creeks snarl into monsters. Rivers doomed to summer meandering become dignified streams, reminiscent of the days before man converted them into polluted conduits for waste.

It is too early for serious cultivation or gardening. The soil is still held by the lingering breath of winter and man can only work it lightly. He is unable to create life, and since April is the month of life and rebirth, he can only wait.

6 *Man and May*

THE MARK OF MAN

On warm Sundays the outward bound city cars spin off the super highways and nose down quiet, country roads. The drivers, usually husbands, are accompanied by observers, wives who scan the surroundings like anxious prospectors looking for a strike.

"Stop, there's one!"

The lode is usually an impromptu flea market, a village second-hand store or simply the roadside stand of a rural entrepreneur selling the contents of attic, basement or woodshed.

Almost any article associated with our pioneer ancestors is considered valuable by these new collectors. Butter bowls, cradles, rockers, churns, stools, benches, samplers, quilts and bedspreads are bought without hesitation. Toted back, the articles mingle somewhat incongruously with products of a plastic and polythene age.

A girl in a modern pad, where the walls blaze with psyche-delic posters, denied that the mixture was "camp or mod."

"It's something different," she said almost wistfully, finger-ing the rough carve marks on the wooden grain scoop she was using as a server, "it's like somebody really cared when they made this. It just didn't pop out of a machine without the mark of a man on it like this other stuff."

VACANT LOTS

A serious casualty in the battle for diminishing city space is the vacant lot. Once plentiful, they have now vanished under apartment buildings and service stations. Children, who found adventure, and the poor, who used them for community centres, suffer the most by their elimination.

The vacant lot was the setting for the free forming of social relationships away from the rigidity of playgrounds. Gangs, groups, clans and clubs, with their individual rewards, flour-ished in these surroundings.

"Sand lot" baseball had a verve impossible to find in adult organized affairs. A boy learned attack as the best defence when friction massaged tempers. He developed skills in trans-forming junk and scrap into clubhouse sanctuaries.

He found tolerance for the cast-off and the unfortunate, who taught him how to use a blade of grass for a whistle or the way to construct a sling-shot from a forked stick and a piece of inner tube. He heard stories of travel and war that remained long after school lessons on the same subjects. Most important, he divined the deception of appearances.

There was common sadness when the hoardings shrouded a vacant lot. There were, however, plenty of others waiting to be colonized. Today this situation is changed. In the modern city there is little regard for the unadorned, unantiseptic and impromptu joys of the young and the poor. Cities are becom-ing more and more places for grown-ups and the rich, for whom a vacant lot is an eyesore denoting a lack of progress.

REWARDS OF MAY

May is a month of reward for the walker. The world is full of the glory of awakened nature. Bulbs burst into splendid bloom, responding to the attention of the patient gardener. The pink and white profusion of fruit blossoms is a mere by-product of creating fleshy containers for fertile seeds.

The misting green of the trees develops imperceptibly and then canopies into full foliage at the touch of a warm sun. Grass tufts and then spreads into a lush carpet. The lilacs, indomitable even in the face of neglect, erupt into flower, filling the air with a heady fragrance.

There are other rewards as well. Now is the time to investigate the earthy, damp mysteries of the swales and swamps. Here the golden flowers of the marsh marigold (Caltha Palustris) bloom in profusion against the dark leaves. Your ancestors gathered those leaves before the blooms appeared and used them as a potherb called "cowslip greens."

Move to the edge of the bushlands where it is still cool in the shade. Here there has been a succession of vivid visitors from hepatica to trilliums and now the amusing preacher flower reigns. Sometimes called Indian turnip because legend says the Indians roasted the roots for food, they are better known as jack-in-the-pulpits. The striped hood, like a curved canopy, protects the cluster of tiny flowers on a green thumb called a spadix. That's Jack, woodland preacher and cousin to such strange relatives as the skunk cabbage and the calla lily.

Listen carefully and you may hear him reminding us with fundamentalist vigor of the debt we owe Nature for beauty as well as careful planning in the rewarding month of May.

HILLS

As a special endowment of our area, hills are a never-ending source of enjoyment. The heritage of geological upheaval, they give evidence that the chance of nature outrivals the most careful landscaping of man.

Now is the time when the everlasting hills seem to flow with subtle greening shades of spring. Topping a hill the traveller is compelled to stop and look in breathless wonder at the panorama. The valley is a place of streams, woods, houses, barns and churches, contrasted with the checkerboard of tilled and untilled fields.

We remember hills. Stubby, fat hills contrast with gaunt, scarred ones where lumbermen have slashed tall timbers, leaving only young trees clutching at minute pockets of soil among the rocks.

Gently rising hills are interlaced by straggling roads as memorials to original Indian trails. There are mysterious outcroppings that always seem wreathed in veils of mist or smoke. Wild apple and chokecherry trees dotted the grassy hillside slopes of childhood.

There is something hauntingly evocative about even the expression concerning the hills of home.

BACK TO THE CAVE

If you can't join your children in their search for tribal society the only way appears to be that of going them one better. Get back to the days of the caveman! Never mind the beads and ornaments and the shoulder-length hair. Skins and pelts will do the trick.

A new fur coat for Prime Minister Trudeau coincides with a male fashion note that to be "in" the executive must sport a coat of pelts of some kind in the coming winter. But that's only part of the story. Caveman styles in more complex ways are bound to happen.

The Wall Street Journal says fur rugs will flourish, helped along by sales to executives who will use them in planes and boats as well as in ski-lodges and cars. Zebra, fox and guanaco will be given top acceptance. Some of the executives plan on surprising their wives with wall-to-wall mink bedroom carpets.

Behind the trend, maintains fur dealer Jacques Kaplan, is

a "subconscious need to go back to a primitive time." Let's see a protesting generation top that one!

TIME OF INDIGNATION

As the traditional call of "sap's running" is heard throughout the land, we enter the time of indignation about youth. The headlines will scream about how vacationing youngsters resist police and become involved in riots. The story will be told from the lawman's point of view, because these spring "mating rites" in cities and towns with a temperate Easter climate, are seldom reported in an unbiased manner.

The high school and college students pour in from the winter-locked northern cities in their jalopies, new cars and motorcycles. It's a co-educational holiday, and, as Lawrence Lipton points out, the literal sense of that statement is learning together. It's a mating rite, in the same sense as the coming out party at the hotel or country club. If the debutante affair gets out of hand, and they have on occasion, wealthy fathers are standing by, with wallets at the ready, to repair the damage.

At the sun and sand affair, parents are missing. Local elders, probably frustrated in their own right, since modern custom forbids them from whipping their own children, are vigilant to call the police for what they consider excess. Blaring radios or phonographs, and empty beer cans send them to the telephone.

So, the police move in with their authority, their night sticks and their tear gas and, what must be apparent, their role of acting for "absentee parents." There is every reason to suspect that this is when the riot starts, and in the manner of reporting since newspapers started covering police beats, the desk sergeant's blotter report gets on the national wire.

An AP story from a small Kansas town where sports car races were to be held was headlined:

"OFFICER DIES, 100 INJURED IN WILD YOUTH MELEE IN QUIET KANSAS TOWN."

Lipton points out in his book *The Erotic Revolution* that the officer died of a heart attack after firing a tear gas shell at the crowd. Similarly, reports that say "thirty thousand or fifty thousand youths in a riot" make us think of a re-enactment of the battle of Dienbienphu. When it's all over, sober reporting of the aftermath invariably shows that riot charges are dismissed or withdrawn, and a token group is charged with "resisting arrest."

Without disparaging the policeman, it must be remembered that he is in the forefront of meeting a problem which most parents have abdicated. He responds to an appeal and moves in, probably with fear, and certainly with the prejudice of his upbringing and training, to face a mass of youth. Ask him, "What do you think of these kids?" and you will hear the response of the average middle-aged North American male.

"No sense of responsibility . . . . I had to work during my holidays and look at the money these kids have to spend . . . . They're nothing but beatniks with long hair . . . . They're juvenile delinquents!"

The final and telling complaint will be, "They won't listen to their parents. They should be horse-whipped."

Who are they really?

They are the objects of the greatest campaign of advertising in existence. For instance, a motivational research group tells the teenage girl, "Excellence in cosmetics causes more comment as a rule and yields greater authority than excellence in scholastic achievements."

Teenagers are involved in the educational process, now becoming the most important dollar industry in North America, as it gropes its way into the electronic age. This is often obscured by the diligence of a principal banning mini-skirts on the grounds of classroom distraction, overlooking the obvious fact that a pretty girl in any attire can be a distraction in a classroom at any time, and especially in the spring.

They are television babies, exposed to electronic communication for ten years or more, opposed to chicness and commercialism, interested in, but not necessarily using, psychedelic substances. Youth opposes sexual mores which they feel are hypocritically guarded by a combination of religion and law, completely bankrupt of anything but outworn Puritanism.

These young people feel that the press is a conservative reflection of the wishes of the establishment. Similarly, the mass communications media such as radio and television are accused of being dominated by sponsors and anxious to not disturb the customers, who in this case are the somewhat confused parents of North America.

In music, art, films and so on, the youth are reaching for their own world and it pre-dates our literate and visual one. Their gatherings at Fort Lauderdale or Bermuda or California resemble what McLuhan calls the "global village." It is tribal and, as Dr. McLuhan says, "Almost any teenager can acquire from his environment masses of data that are utterly beyond his professors. They live in a world in which classified categories are meaningless, and dispensing with the accepted methods of looking at things appeals to them."

In any case, these same members of a new generation will in a few years be the leaders of the community. They will have to deal with air and water pollution, with our disorganized and dying cities, with overwhelming adjustments in transportation, with over-population control and feeding, with education and all its facets and with how to adjust to computer technology and leisure. Forty years ago we marvelled at primitive telephone, radio and telegraph communication. They will be using globe-spanning satellites and instant communication, to say nothing of inter-space travel and communication.

If you have questions about this generation, try and talk to them. They have doubts about our generation, its sincerity and even its competence.

DANCING MAY FLIES

The art of tying artificial flies predates even *The Compleat Angler* of Izaak Walton by 168 years. A woman, Dame Julian

Berners, prioress of Sopwell Abbey, composed the first manual on the subject in *The Book of Saint Albans* in 1485.

The fisherman waiting by a quiet pool in May for the mysterious cycle of the may fly (Ephemerideae) may discount this as a fallacy. A winter of tying and retying the lures will have confirmed it to be a male prerogative.

Hatching from eggs laid last May, the nymphs remained at the bottom of the water. Now they break the surface and, splitting their dull armor, get airborne on clumsy wings. At that moment the fisherman casts, hoping to fool the wily trout.

It's a brief contest, because the awkward flies dance and wobble and move, if they escape fish and birds, to the bank bushes. Here a new transformation takes place as the temporary equipment is replaced by gauzy wings which are more efficient and graceful. The may flies then soar high and mate. Soon after, the male flutters down to perish, and the females remain only long enough to lay their eggs for next year's brief appearance.

For the fisherman it is a moment of excitement and deep appreciation if his flies lure a quota of fish to his line and tackle. The naturalist knows it as another of those wondrous moments in the eternal pattern of nature.

In less congested days, the may flies went back to die in the water, a source of food and material in the cycle. Now that man has taken over beach and waterfront for his own purposes, the crowds of dying adults become a nuisance. Expo officials, for instance, could be pardoned for feeling less than enthusiastic about this miracle of nature. It may account for the reason fishermen call them may flies, while others are inclined to use the less graceful sounding term, shad flies!

FREEDOM OF DRESS

While the Royal Commission on the Status of Women dutifully tallies grievances of a male-dominated society, one phenomenon of female determination becomes more apparent.

Female thighs and knees, released from imprisonment in the wrappings of fashion, remain in the open.

The mini-skirt bows to neither Montreal winters nor fashion dictates. Designers cajole and suggest everything from voluminous caftans and djellabas to the swirling wraps of the Bonnie and Clyde era, but female appendages still cling to their place in the sun.

In this day of "electronic environment" they have subscribed to the cool message of non-concealment of the medium. Girls display everything, from pencil-like stalks to smooth, linear development and even startling sets of parenthesis, secure in the knowledge that the North American male is often more strongly attracted by reality than abstraction.

DESERTED FARM

A deserted farm is a sad memorial at any time, but it seems tragic in May. This is the month when the country is full-fashioned with the delight of bloom and blossom, and the vacancy is startling and wasteful in the face of the spring yearnings of so many caught in the sterility of urban congestion.

The orchard may be gnarled and twisted from winter lashings and frost tantalizings, but the brave old trees, in spite of neglect, show their blossoms like proud veterans at a reunion. Here the busybody bees fuss in and out, collecting nectar and at the same time spreading the pollen, so that by harvest time there will at least be fruit of some kind with fertile seeds to carry on nature's work.

The gaunt house with its empty eye sockets of windows has the loyal protection of the proliferating lilacs, screening it with masses of purple and white blooms from roadside stares. Stubby rose bushes are back in life, unkempt like neglected children. Here and there, flowers still bloom. These patient mourners are unable to believe that the mistress of the house will never come back.

Under the tangled remains of weeds, there appear strange, mutated remnants of a vegetable garden. A broken hoe, rusted and warped, lies as if waiting for hands to pick it up and begin over again.

If you listen carefully past the humming activity of birds and insects, you can almost hear the sounds of the farmer and his family. It's all expectant, in the way of nature, where each tenure is but a short interval in the eternal cycle of death and renewal, for man to begin a new pattern of co-operation.

A SPECIAL TREE

A particular tree often stands out in memory. It may be the spreading, comfortable one that gave shelter from rain or shade from hot sun on daily school treks.

Climbing trees had convenient access by way of lower branches for children anxious to emulate Tarzan after a Saturday movie. Every backyard seemed to have a tree with a branch for a swing.

You may remember the tree where you carved initials to record undying adolescent love. Others enshrine a tree because for them it was associated with a more permanent love that didn't require advertising.

In later life, special trees catch our fancy in different ways. One seems ideal for a landscape. Another mirrors the sun from dawn to dusk.

There may be deeper significance. A favorite tree comes pulsing into spring life of sap and buds. Finally it is covered by greenery and becomes a haunt of birds and a place of shade for a man in a serene summer. Then comes fall. The tree displays the full regalia of a passing-out ceremony with autumnal color, like an old soldier on final parade.

We wait, as helpless as the tree itself, in the face of nature's mustering-out, for the long, naked sleep of winter.

THE WINDOW BOX

From tatty tenement to apartment sepulchre, the window box is a bright splash of courage against urban drabness and sterility. It is the protest mark of the individual in the face of corporate indifference.

The institutionally imprisoned cherish a single weed or flower as a symbol of freedom. Likewise, the window box gardener may remember an open childhood of brightness and space. There is a renewal of simple faith in the power of growing things.

The miniscule plot of land stirs root depths of the age old affinity of man and soil. There is above all the mystery of the seed, still complex and baffling to men who have released the secret of the atom.

On a summer evening when the city relaxes from the hot chaos of day, the reward comes for the window box owner. The soil drinks deeply, the leaves glisten and the blooms are radiant. Musky land scents and blossom fragrances for a short time counteract the acidity of polluted air from the canyoned streets.

A man can anticipate as well an early morning visit from a vibrant humming-bird.

In the face of this, how . . . oh how can anyone resort to the artificiality of adorning a window box with those shoddy symbols of progress, plastic flowers and foliage?

7 *June and Things*

SCENTED MONTH

June is a scented month. It is the perfumed courtesan of the year, beguiling with fragrances powerful enough to make the most conscientious waver in his routine.

Routine is unknown to this adventurous period of the year. It comes in tantalizingly with the delicate spice of the narcissi and lilies of the valley. There is something almost, but not quite, vulgar in the abundance with which the lilacs load the evening air.

Then comes the hay sap, oozing at the fresh knife cuts of the mower. In the glare of the hot sun it smells peppery, and at night it has in its essence all the poignancy of a country-man's memory.

The final blow to sensibility and routine comes with the roses. Since they originated as seafoam at the birth of Aphrodite, and have been linked to Eros, the Muses and the Graces, the sight and smell of roses is enough to put the mark of pagan abandonment on June.

It is a brave, or perhaps only a foolish man, who resists the call to enjoy a scented month.

TYRANNY OF GRASS

This is the time of year when suburban man wonders about the value of one status symbol — the front lawn. In the first flush of spring enthusiasm he raked, rolled, spudded, fertilized and pampered the tiny plot. There was an almost mystical quality to his renewal of a partnership with nature.

As the grass responded to his ministrations and the sun grew more intense, his zeal began to wane. Yet he couldn't abdicate. Sitting on the patio there were the ever-present sounds of busy neighbors as reminders. The suggestion from his wife that he place a sign out front reading "Wilderness Acres" sends him back to the fray.

The harassed householder will find at this point that neighborhood youth is apparently no longer hungry for pocket money. If he bribes or bullies them into manicuring the plot, they will be certain to leave jagged ridges which will demand as much attention as if he had cut the grass in the first place. Professional gardeners who accept the work will devote equal time to campaigning for the job of landscaping the entire lot.

If he yields to a doctor's warning about undue exercise and buys a power mower, his business instincts will tell him his investment is sufficient for a market gardener. When he produces the equipment, the man across the street will appear with one which has a seat for the driver.

The home owner begins to dream of desperate things such as importing a goat, buying artificial grass like that used by the local undertaker, or walling the area in with a paved courtyard like a Roman home. Then he is spared by vacation time and he departs with the problem unsolved, but mercifully out of sight.

THE WILD ROSE

Nature has a way of dressing up normally unattractive spots. Berry bushes flourish where man leaves a pile of trash after timber slashing. Moss and ivy cling and cluster to soften the rawness of jagged rock or the remnants of a building foundation.

In June you find the wild roses. Often called sweetbrier, the delicate flowering bush came from Europe where it was known as eglantine. In our area there are several varieties, often called pasture or swamp roses by countrymen.

The wild rose is by design a creation of the outdoors. Protected by scratchy briers, the delicate blooms soon wilt if clipped. Children learn this to their dismay when attempting to take a bouquet of wild roses home to mother.

In June the wild rose belongs to the fragrant world of growth. They are to be admired in their surroundings.

JUNE RAIN

Man, beast and earth welcome the steady June rain that comes pouring from the night sky. Thunder grumbles but keeps a distance. An occasional whiplash of lightning sears the darkness. Coolness comes to push away the daytime clamminess.

Windows open and stay that way because this is a precise downpour without a distracting breeze. Sleepers come awake from fitful rest, reach for covers and subconsciously are appreciative of the blessed coolness in the benediction of the rain.

This time of June night rain is a jewelled period, when the city dweller has a relatively clean surrounding. It's soon obliterated by the fumes and noise, and we can only wonder at how splendid a city could be, if man only relaxed his campaign against the natural amenities.

JUNE

Poets have by no means exhausted the potential of June.

Without mentioning the moon, there's inspiration in all kinds of magical activity.

Why do birds seem stereophonic at dusk and dawn? What gives hushed mystery and somehow cleaner-seeming air to the noisiest city on a warm, June night? Where is there a human who doesn't pause at least for a moment to think of less hectic times while under the spell of lilac or rose perfume?

It's a month of yearning for students as they mentally erase the calendar days until spring freedom. It's a time of vexation for suburban lawn-makers as they note the invasion of their expensively cultivated plots by legions of quack grass and bindweed.

June is still the month we have been waiting for. From the countryman watching his greening fields to the city man dallying over the purchase of a power boat, it is a month that stirs a joyous song in the hearts of all.

TAKES TWO TO TELEPHONE

The telephone is a wonderful convenience. I've stood in awe of it ever since the first one shattered the isolation of my childhood farm home.

The telephone has become a nuisance. This has happened largely because door-to-door salesmen have discovered that the regular directory, as well as the yellow one, can do their walking for them. The result is a continual barrage of people calling with a sales pitch. A ringing telephone is the enemy of inspiration for a writer, because, as Mignon McLaughlin puts it, "Creative work is one of life's greatest pleasures, and the only one we will gladly interrupt."

I can't ignore a telephone call. It may be possible to overlook the first few "braangs," but by the fifth or sixth I'm dashing with apologies for being slow.

A dangling receiver puts an unknown factor in the house. It's so easy to imagine all sorts of important calls being blocked by the disconnected instrument. Someone may be sick! An old friend is just passing through town and keeps trying to get the number. I always yield to the inner turmoil and replace the receiver, and sure enough the first call will be someone trying to sell something.

The unlisted telephone has always seemed to me an affectation. Part of this prejudice comes from spending hours trying to locate an individual only to find him hiding behind the barrier of an unlisted number. Then, after an hour's taxi ride, you discover that he had gone to Florida or the United Kingdom.

Recently I tried fighting back against the pests who call after random selection of names in the telephone directory. It went something like this:

"Sir, I am allowed to offer you a thirty-three and a third — that's one third, mind you — discount on new aluminum storm windows for this week only. A representative will call without obligation if you are interested?"

"How dare you?"

The unknown voice grew apprehensive.

"I beg your pardon."

"I am Henry J. Kaiser's brother-in-law."

After a few gulps the caller hung up. This strengthened my belief that people impaled by telephone callers don't talk back. I was ready for the next one.

"Sir, to what radio station or television station are you tuned at the moment?"

"KDKA, Pittsburgh, Pennsylvania."

I was old enough to remember those pioneer days of broadcasting, but honey voice on the other end of the line was slightly stumped.

"Ah . . . . er . . . . ah . . . . yes, sir. What program is that?"

"The A. & P. Gypsies."

She mumbled something unintelligible and hung up. I was elated. This was more fun than putting extra holes in computerized reply cards.

Heady with success, I assured an encyclopedia salesman that I would shill in the neighborhood to introduce his books, if he gave me a dozen free copies of Fanny Hill for my friends. I assured a contact for the Ontario Motor League that I had no use for its emergency service because I still drove a horse and buggy.

A somewhat nervous voice with a trace of foreign accent wanted to know my breakfast habits.

"Sir, I am sorry to trouble you, but do you enjoy your breakfast?"

"I certainly do."

This gave her confidence.

"May I ask what brand of breakfast cereal you enjoy?"

"Never touch the stuff."

There was genuine grief in her voice.

"Oh, no cereal."

"I am a follower of the J. Paul Getty formula for breakfast."

This interested her, so I continued:

"Oysters, caviar, a little Melba toast and black velvet."

Before I could tell her black velvet was a combination of champagne and stout she hung up. I couldn't work, but at least I was getting some satisfaction out of the calls. I sat there trying to anticipate what the next call would be about. A deep-voiced, sincere-sounding man called.

"Mr. Boyle, I am Tom Jones of Litmus Realty. We have just completed a very favorable sale in your district."

He waited I suppose for my congratulations, but I stayed silent.

"Mr. Boyle, I am pleased to say we have a client interested in your home."

He paused for effect but I stayed mum.

"Might I ask, would you be interested in selling your home."

I, too, used the pregnant pause.

"No, I am not going to sell. Taxes and government foolishness have brought me to the point where rather than sell I am going to take drastic action."

I paused and he bit.

"What?"

"I am going to blow the whole shebang sky-high."

He slammed the receiver down but I didn't mind. This was a real triumph, and I had just started to work at writing when a police cruiser appeared, nosing slowly along the street. It went past and then came back, and as my heart started pounding it stopped in front of my house. A tall young officer got out, looked carefully at my car on the street and the number of the house, and then rang the bell. Policemen terrify me any time, and with none of the repartee which I had used on the telephone at my command, I opened the door.

"Sir," he said, "I thought I better tell you that you left on the lights on your car. Run down a battery that way."

I don't know what I stammered as he turned away, but as I turned off the car lights, I made a resolution to forget the prejudice and get an unlisted telephone number.

SONG BIRDS

Very few people in North America would tolerate the indiscriminate killing of a bird. Most will take steps to thwart a cat stalking a robin. Yet there seems little concern over the increasing and extravagant use of poison sprays and insecticides which pose serious hazards to the bird population.

It is estimated that fifteen billion birds spend some part of each year in North America. They are a vital part of the ecological pattern, helping in ways which make the whole insecticide method of controlling insects seem a puny thing.

Once we have scientific developments such as poison sprays there can be no hope of turning back. Caution against the control agent itself becoming a killer and destroyer must be exercised.

If this constant check on abuse is not made, future generations may live in a time without birds or their songs.

COMMUNICATIONS

Adults who bemoan the lack of successful relationships with their children might be rewarded if they tried listening in place of telling for a change. A grade eight student in Toronto has defined the communications problem in *The Christian Way of Life* for her final examination.

She wrote:

> "Good communications among the human race is scarce because of racial discrimination and the graded human being (rich, poor, average). Many children are discouraged from making friends with a person of another race or even a different class (rich, poor). These children never have and probably never will, a chance to communicate with others no matter what race or religion, for they create a prejudice because of their parents' forcefulness."

DROPOUT!

"Everything was bad about our son dropping out of school and going hippie," says Peter M., a Toronto business executive. "It was a trauma for my wife and a jolt for me! I have to be honest about this. I'm not certain the whole thing wasn't a blast at our pride more than concern for the boy. But it was a good thing for us!"

Henry was sixteen. He had been complaining about school, objecting to haircuts, staying out late and acting in a "surly" way. He balked at going to Jasper for a summer holiday.

"I put this down to age. Growing up! Let's face it, Jasper is not a swinging place. We went because our friends were there. My father had gone there because he was a railroad executive. Henry said he wanted to study for the fall. When we came back he was gone. He left a note saying he was going to try and find himself."

The parents were annoyed but not alarmed.

"We had not really been close to him. My wife was a volunteer worker at charity and that sort of thing and I had a lot of business engagements. We have a country place. It's a farm that's not very posh. I intended to build a decent country house but never got around to it. My wife was worried, but I hated to go to the police. We went up to the farm two weeks later. Henry had been there all the time and must have just got out ahead of us."

Henry had not been alone. The neighbors said several boys and girls, whom they described as "long haired and dirty," had been staying at the house. This, plus the evidence in the house of a bohemian existence, sent Peter's wife into orbit with anxiety.

"I went to the police. They found him and brought him home. It was desperate. He was different. Now, that's what we wanted to think. We later found out we didn't know our son really. There was no communication at all. It was a nightmare. He was not going back to school. We were all 'squares' who didn't understand him or his generation. The world was a dreadful place and he didn't want to join the 'rat race.'"

A comedy of tragedies followed. He stayed in his room and refused to eat. Later he vanished and this time the police couldn't find him.

"I had to take serious stock of the situation," says Peter. "What was the sense of dragging him back? I went to a doctor and he shrugged his shoulders and admitted he had a daughter and a son, both threatening to leave home. A community worker chastised me as being the cause of Henry's leaving home because of a lack of relationship."

A psychiatrist suggested he bring the boy to him, and he would try to get his confidence.

"That's what put the idea in my head. Confidence. If the psychiatrist had to find a way to gain his confidence, couldn't I try the same thing. After all, I had some advantages."

The parent started moving at night into the areas where he thought the hippies would congregate.

"I went to coffee houses and listened to wild music and watched psychedelic lights until I was almost blind. No sign of Henry. One night I asked a young man who was older than the usual group, if there was any way of locating him. He asked me for a description, told me to go home and called me two days later. I went to a house and there was Henry with a group of others, sick and dreadful looking."

Peter had been warned by the go-between not to press the point.

"I just asked him if there was anything he needed. He said no and I went home. It was hard to do. Two days later his mother called and said he was at home. She was almost hysterical but hadn't exploded in front of Henry. For a month, he was at home and then we would forget ourselves and start the old moralizing bit . . . . and he would go away. But he was coming home more often and changing his clothes and taking long baths and eating a bit. Once he brought home some of the wildest characters I've ever seen. I must say by this time my wife was learning because she set out food for them and endured the hi-fi blasting out music that . . . she, well . . . didn't appreciate!"

Peter said conversation was difficult. Henry was rebelling and couldn't articulate the source of his rebellion. The boy smoked marijuana at home; he was tempted to try it, but satisfied himself by not scolding.

"Henry kept saying there was a conspiracy against youth. Older people were against young people. Then, one day, by something he said, I discovered he had been touched by the fact I went looking for him. Felt a bit guilty! He knew we cared for him and dammit, I knew we hadn't shown him much affection since he was a baby."

Peter puzzled over it, and then remembered the small farm.

"I persuaded my wife we needed to get away for a time and I asked Henry how he would like to come and help me fix the place up a bit. I didn't say it, but I inferred I was fed up with the rat race. I was, too. He had influenced me. Well, he came and I think he thought it was a trick at first, but within two weeks it was a new world. We somehow did some carpenter work and plumbing and the two months went like magic. How did it end? Happy, I would say. He went back to school . . . a vocational school because he wants to work with his hands. I've cut down on my business work and we spend a lot of time in the country. It's still touchy but my wife and I learned one thing. When these young people say they want to be useful, they mean it. Their trouble is finding a way."

SUMMER

A century before Chaucer a poet wrote:

"Summer is icumen in,
    Lhude sing cuccu."

Now it is upon us, this season that holds delight for everyone from school-released child to office refugee. It brings hot weather, the same atmosphere Canadians seek so assiduously by southern exposure during winter.

Yet the summer has handicaps in this modern age of improvement and development. The song of the cuckoo is scarce, but many will protest in vain about the increasing tendencies of starlings to spend their days raiding country fields and their noisy evenings in the thick sanctuary of suburban trees.

Gardeners in hot weather find spring enthusiasm wearing thin as their plots are invaded by bindweed, thistles, chickweed, purslane, mullin, lamb's quarters and quack grass. Farmers will be tempted to surrender to the advancing forces of chicory, spurge and mustard.

Ardent fishermen, toting a winter's accumulation of new equipment piled in the repainted boat and trailer, may search for clean, fresh, free-flowing streams. The search will be more difficult as the menace of pollution spreads, suggesting apathy and selfishness in the face of common sense.

Weekend vacationers will clog traffic arteries and main

roadways on Friday and Saturday nights. The stalled pleasure-seeker may wonder wistfully if his new leisure and freedom isn't in some ways a mockery.

The truth is, it's still summer. There are table pleasures of sheer delight in a home-grown meal. Fishing spots and wilderness areas are being guarded against selfish encroachment. Whippoorwills and loons sound their plaintive calls at dusk across cool, dark northern waters.

Summer is here in full glory. Enjoy it!

8   *The Spirit and the Flame*

There is hope in the fact that our Ottawa Centennial flame continues to burn, symbolic of the Canadian spirit. People were really concerned when it appeared as if it would be doused. It looked suspiciously as if official Canada didn't realize just how optimistic the genie was that they released in 1967.

Max Ferguson, an amusing man who carries concealed weapons of satire in his sketches on CBC radio, may have had something to do with it. When it looked as if the flame was going to be extinguished, he had Prime Minister Pearson introduce a new feature with the blackout. The runners who one year earlier had been sent out with blazing torches would, on the eve of a New Year, proceed over the same routes with unlit ones.

Ferguson didn't explain. He may have been poking fun at Sharpian dictums for economies. On the other hand, he was no doubt pointing up the Canadian trick of officialdom with brave words about the shining, burning future but acting out the old myth that for every success we have in Canada we are bound to suffer, pay or have a setback.

Someone must have said, "T'ain't necessarily so!" He is right.

The youth of this country doesn't believe in a setback. They have no tiresome memories of depression or idolatrous feelings for the United States. In fact, the alarming trends in America of an establishment gearing to engender support in the name of patriotism for an unfortunate war is withering whatever attraction they may have felt for that country.

Canada began the Centennial Year with an attitude somehow like that of Mexico in its pre-revolutionary days, so far from God and so near the United States. It left the year with a much clearer sense of perspective as far as the deity is concerned, and with a feeling of accomplishment which leaves the United States a neighbor, in place of a holy Mecca, for those wanting commercial success.

We discovered, in large part from the Expo experience, that if there is any hope of making contact with the spirit of creation, then it must begin in our relationships with individual man. Young people, and an amazing number of older people as well, feel that inherited prides, which are often only snobberies, must not stand in the way of putting our domestic house in order. We can then proceed to the task of forming attitudes conducive to making the term "brotherhood of man" more than simply an excuse for jaded consciences on the international banquet circuit.

The confluence of people on Canada in 1967 impressed the average citizen very much. Taken in conjunction with an overriding theme "man and his world," it had a powerful effect on us as individuals. We have something to contribute and the world needs our services. We are a people of good fortune. Secure in wealth and physical assets that we have not yet plundered beyond rectification, we have a responsibility to share our good fortune.

Poised on the verge of massive urbanization, we still have a chance to build with concern for the individual. We still have an opportunity to allow ourselves to live in dignity without loneliness. If we can now apply our skills to the cause of environmental security, in the way we have to social services, there is hope we may supply our children with security of the spirit, the one absolute necessity for a world endowed with leisure.

Again we know it can be done. We saw it in action during Centennial year. It requires foresight on the part of leaders. There has to be a constant vigilance against the selfishness of expediency and privilege, so that our cities and towns will be designed for the comfort, peace and tranquility of all men, in place of being jungles of discordancy, pollution and disharmony.

People of influence in this country have to stop being chameleon creatures. In their homes and their home surroundings they are good citizens, trying to raise their children and help in the community. They are filled with the same disgust as everyone else for municipalities which are seemingly impotent to do anything about such problems as pollution. Yet these same men when they travel from their homes to their offices become co-operating parts of the corporate, business and political organizations which tolerate the impossible situations.

The miracle of Expo for me was the fact that the people responsible kept their concern. They started with the theme of man and his world and all it entailed, and they persevered so that man did not take a second place to his toys whether they were automobiles or noise-makers.

I will remember as long as I live the statement of a 37-year-old man from Quebec City. He had started as a travelling salesman when he was quite young and he was interviewed as he left the Christian pavilion:

"I was tired, you know, the way you get when you're coming up to middle age and you have been working a long time. I started out going from small place to small place and staying in little hotels, and most of them were dirty and not very well kept up. They are just depressing and our villages in Quebec have been getting to look like just so many other places in North America, with all kinds of old signs and service stations and nothing, really, what you might say, was for the soul."

He had come to the islands in the St. Lawrence, not as a pilgrim with great hopes, but just because it was the thing to do.

"But now I feel different. People say that the film in the church pavilion is depressing. I don't think so at all. I think it makes me feel good that there is so much we can do in Canada to help people who have it very bad."

About his tiredness of spirit he was joyful:

"I am staying a week and I am going to come back for a week. It is not only the exhibitions. They are interesting. It is being able to sit down and look at the river and over at Montreal and see the people around, and today I was invited to join a family from India. They had those little flat cakes, like our pancakes . . . flans . . . and it was wonderful. I was proud . . . not only proud of being a Quebecois . . . and proud of Montreal and Jean Drapeau . . . but more, I was really proud when they said those nice things about Canada. I had never thought much about this before."

A 21-year-old from Ghana related how he had followed the progress of Expo on short-wave radio. He knew a lot about our music and musicians and wanted desperately to meet Gordon Lightfoot, the singer and song writer, and Moe Kauffman, who composed "The Swinging Shepherd Blues." Now, in the aftermath of the event when we are busy extinguishing torches and being practical, I wondered what David would think about plans to curtail the short wave broadcasting facilities.

"Man," I can just hear and picture him exclaiming, "man, you must just be crazy or something. We like Canada and we listen. We just want you to tell us more."

Listen, Ottawa, listen to what a 12-year-old girl, Kate Hamilton found in just one exhibit:

"The Mexican pavilion dealt with people, long ago people and people now, and people in between, but they were all one people, continuous. People that died in the hills centuries ago after leaving something, a great golden shrine, magnificent, both from a distance and close; a carving in rock like the Egyptian hieroglyphics (these were very detailed and most people looked onto the closet size rooms and saw emptiness with pretty wallpaper, but I found kings and queens and slaves and fights and winners and losers and joy and death and life). There were beautiful wooden Christs, looking so real and so hurting that I heard one woman say she wanted to wipe His face and dress His wounds. Then, down a flight of stairs, I came face to face with lovely, lively, happy, modern art. Saying HI!"

To her this was no once in a lifetime miracle. This was for her a real world, the world of today; and economics and all the nostalgic pessimism it is possible to conjure up will not convince her and her like that she doesn't deserve a world of environmental pleasantness.

In April of 1967 I was willing to admit that Canadians were a private kind of people. It's no longer so. At least I will say that fifty per cent of our population under twenty-five are not emotionally isolationist. In fact, a surprising number of an older generation have had the comfortable supports pulled out from under their postures.

We were scarcely out of the aura of Expo before the old French-English question popped up. I am sure that it was pushed into the forefront at this particular time by many who feared the strange fusion of interests effected by Centennial and Expo. On the face of it, there can be little doubt that many of the regional politicians are still motivated by the old myths. It's too bad more of them hadn't been forced to stand in line at Expo. They would have found there a grass roots communication, the like of which this country has never seen before, and which had better soon start motivating our national instruments of communication. This was dialogue that did more to break down fallacies about opposing interests than all the arguments politicians of French and English origin have been able to muster since 1867.

But even here there are hopes, apart from the public lessons of the Confederation For Tomorrow Conference. Hubert Prefontaine, 32, is a native of St. Boniface, a self-made man and a consultant in economics. He is a member of that other force, the people of French ancestry who live outside the physical boundaries of Quebec. He was a delegate to the Estates-General conference and lived painful moments at it, saying that for those few days he felt like a stranger in his own country. He labels the forces of independence as real, with reasonable positions yielding to radical and inflexible attitudes based almost entirely on emotion. He called it "a striking contrast of collective power and cultural despair."

On a CBC-TV broadcast of *Viewpoint*, he stated what he felt was a solution:

"The solution of the French language problem is not enough. I believe that for establishment of a real Canadian unity it is essential that we develop exciting national goals, based on the fundamental worth of each and every human being, as Quebec itself has shown us. We need some powerful common causes. We could tackle the injustice wrought upon our Indian population. We could provide major food and assistance programs for starving nations. We could develop our national goals into something meaningful for a large number of our young people. We could develop less degrading approaches to welfare and the relief of poverty and alienation. We could do all of these and many more, with a real participation of a large number of our people in all parts of Canada.

"The great forces developing in Quebec must be channelled against the common enemies of our nation: waste, poverty, hunger, greed, and servile dependence. Indirectly the people of Quebec are challenging us to the building of a better society.

And I am convinced that only in this way can we find the potential for a national unity built upon deep ideals rather than superficial structures."

It can be done. We are no longer a lonely people, constantly diminished by recollection of space and dominated by the images of two shining tracks of a transcontinental train system and a five and a half hour time differential. One plane trip is enough to shatter the tyrannical myths of space and time shackles. One trip to Expo was enough to awaken new hopes in the minds and hearts of young people and a significant number of older ones. It gave us the breathless message that somehow fellow Canadians had been able to cast out individual prejudices and isolation to make science and art work for the good of all. It told us that in this there is an abounding hope for the future.

But what about those runners of Max Ferguson's sketch with their unlit torches? Where were they going? Then it all came clear. Hugh MacLennan, lauding Expo and the Centennial, had said, "We are out in the world of man with his long history and mysterious future, at last we are visible in it, and we cannot crawl back into our provincial caves ever again."

Let's hope that official Ottawa is tending the flame because they know and feel in their hearts that Canada's future is too good to be squandered either in the darkness of provincial caves or to be shackled to musty archives reeking of yesterday's pessimisms.

9   *Hot July*

FARM BARNS

By midsummer, farm barns become places of fragrant mystery. They reek with the amber essence of cured timothy hay and the spiciness of clover. Above the mows, sparrows twitter and pigeons burble on endlessly.

There will soon be golden straw bulking beside the brown and green hay. When the granary swells with grain, the stable cats will be attracted by an influx of rodents.

Boards from old barns are now a rage with interior decorators. They appear in everything from chic restaurants to recreation rooms as siding and panelling. One artist selects knotted, weathered or whorled sections and mounts them as pieces of natural art.

There may be artistic merit in aged boards from country barns. More likely people are simply trying to recapture memories of childhood and adolescence, when a farm barn was a place of fun and emotional warmth on a summer day.

DOG DAYS

Star gazers call the time in July when the Dog Star, Sirius, is in conjunction with the sun, the Dog Days. In ancient Rome all kinds of disasters from mad dogs to poisoned water were blamed on the unearthly phenomenon.

Today, when science provides answers unrelated to superstition, we are inclined, in the heat-induced listlessness of a dwindling month, to place at least a token belief in Dog Days. At mid-day with a blazing sun there isn't even the solace of cheerful bird song, for these creatures are wise enough to conserve their energies for dusk and dawn serenades.

Brown drought casts a hot gloom on dry sections and ponds sprout green scum. In some areas rain comes intemperately, flushing off the baked earth, while farmers grow apprehensive for the fragile, supporting stalks of ripening grain.

In oven-like cities men move from the oasis of an air conditioned office to a similar comfort in a bar or restaurant. They postpone — until night brings some relief — returning to homes summer-vacated by their families.

In the country the sweet musk of milkweed rivals the smell of second cut hay. The roadsides froth with the delicate white of tracery of Queen Anne's Lace. The corn flaunts golden tassels. In fence corners and logged-over areas, tangled shrubbery is rank with raspberries waiting for animal, bird or human pickers.

The world is caught in the hot vise of a sun-busy ripening. There is a lesson for every human in how great a temptation it takes to make the family pet move from a sheltered spot. In many ways this is a reasonable enough excuse for us to call them Dog Days.

PICKING BERRIES

This is the time of year when people of country background find a mysterious power luring them to dusty side and back roads. They have fantasies about berries, the wild kind. Not even the most attractive market or store display can shake their desire for a sampling of red, black or thimble berries in the natural state.

Wild berries grow less accessible each year as the highways, subdivisions, and resort areas proliferate. There are simply fewer fence bottoms and old timber slashes left for them to grow in.

Enthusiasts still are able to locate some patches. If you persist, surviving mosquitoes, wasps, brambles and the hostility of country residents, you will be amply rewarded. Wild berries, picked by hand, are an epicurean delight.

Just for a short time, unmindful of scratches, bites and pointed remarks, and with the mouth-tingling flavor, a picker can remember the sun-drenched happiness of a summer childhood.

SUMMER NIGHTS

The discordancies of day are muted in the soft, dark velvet of summer nights. At dusk, gentle breezes come up like cooling fingers to massage away the irritations of harshness left by the day's heat.

On back stoop, veranda or porch, the countryman enjoys the comfort of relaxation from work as a prelude to healing sleep. Pipes glow and smoke wreathes as faces flare into momentary prominence in match flames.

In the dark, silvered twilight, the swallows show their perfection in flying acrobatics. The mysterious bats glide around the buildings blundering into the anomaly of sightlessness when confronted with light, proving that they are truly creatures of darkness.

The splotched pinks and fiery golds of the sun's afterglow linger on reluctantly in the western sky. Suddenly they are put to rout and the mystery of darkness begins. This is an enveloping environment that billows in, pinpricked by the tiny, winking flames of the fireflies.

Noise, the natural enemy of man's contentment, is subdued. Birds whisper in trees while the whippoorwills call plaintively.

The owl is solemn. The passing train creases the silence with rumble and blast, leaving an even greater poignancy in the stillness when it has passed. All around there is the orchestration of tiny sounds of insects and rustling leaves.

It is a time of great satisfaction, designed as a bonus of enjoyment. The countryman leaves it reluctantly for needed rest.

HOLLYHOCKS

Tidy gardens, one of the glories of summer, are now coming into their own in country hamlets and on farms where space is still a convenience of man in place of an economic concern. These are the places where people who prize a partnership with nature find satisfaction physically as well as aesthetically.

These gardeners by mid-summer have experienced the sensation of earthy, new potatoes and slim, crunchy carrots. Crisp lettuce, dew-freshened, provides salad beds for nippy radishes, onions with a hot breath and the first tomatoes, which seem the essence of sun and summer.

The true gardener has, in addition to the delights of taste, an eye for color and beauty. Pansies with shy faces, golden-orange nasturtiums and roses like carved masterpieces contrast with the abundance of geraniums, zinnias and petunias. The cosmos and asters stand in elegant tracery.

The mark of the true gardener is a showing of hollyhocks. Masking a building, serving as a divider or a casual backdrop, the hollyhocks bring their own charm. With their colorful, wrinkled petals and slender but tough stems they are hardy veterans of drought and pest. In a way they represent the gardeners who persist against all obstacles to provide color and necessities in their summer plots.

THE CONFRONTATION

For several summers now, I have been "teaching" creative writing at the Banff School of Fine Arts. Why would twenty-four people of differing ages and backgrounds take time off in the middle of summer to study writing? Why would anyone take classes for a month in a subject which, it is generally agreed, cannot be taught? Will the course be simply an excuse for people to spend a delightful month in the mountains? How many of them will be determined on a career of riches after publishing verse or a story in a local newspaper or a church magazine?

You may be thinking these questions when you arrive at the Banff School of Fine Arts, and then you rediscover the reality of an amazing vitality in Canada. The problem with almost all education, information and communication for those of us who have been in these fields for a number of years is that our rules are the same but the game has changed.

Writing? That's a formal thing. You must have something to say and find the most direct way of saying it. To learn is simply to work until you have discovered and perfected the ability to write what you have to say. That's the rule and it has been since writing became an art!

"But sir," says the eager-eyed youngster with the stiff thatch of hair and the teeth braces gleaming in his sharp face, "what we, I mean I, really want to learn is how do I . . . well . . . how do I get across to someone who isn't of my generation, what I feel?"

There is no need to answer because the minister's wife from a small town in Ontario is in agreement.

"That's exactly it. I went to university. I took all the literature courses. Now I am married to a man who is struggling with the new idea of Christianity and ecumenism and I have four teenage daughters. It may seem silly but I came here to learn or try to learn how to express myself so they will understand."

There's not much use in starting with The Rules For Fiction Writing, Number One! How many more feel the same way? The answers are different in structure but similar in intent.

Terry is shy. He has deliberately fought against it, and when he couldn't make his parents understand he went to work on the Vancouver docks, and holed up in the winter and tried to write, but it wouldn't come.

"All this feeling I have and when I try to get it down it clogs up in me. There are so many misunderstandings we could fix up. I gave up school because it was so irrelevant and when I tried to talk to my teachers they hid behind a course of study."

What do the five school teachers of literature feel about it?

"There are two things wrong. The course of study is a curse to us when we have students we could help, but I also blame the parents for not being interested. It's a case of giving everything in terms of help and money but not having any of themselves to give."

"Students are bored. They've had television sets for baby-sitters and more and more feel what we are trying to tell them is dull. Sometimes they know more than we do."

"You get this glimpse at times into the students of a terrible loneliness. They want someone to talk to who won't be patronizing."

Jacqueline teaches primary school in Northern Alberta.

"It's not sophisticated where I come from but it's hard to stick to what you have to work with, when the youngsters are talking about the thrust of a rocket the way we used to marvel at a new Model A Ford."

Patricia is doe-eyed, dark-haired and reticent.

"I live on a ranch," she says finally. "You know the kind now where we have cars and trucks and all kinds of inter-coms and money and I'm lonely." She says finally, "My ambition is to be a hippy."

Hippies! It had to come out because it somehow represents the symbol of the search for communications between the generations. The older people are not really bitter. It's curiosity more than anything!

"I am puzzled," says the librarian from Nanaimo, leaving for the Northwest Territories because her family has grown up and she's alone and wants to live a bit. "I wish they were cleaner but I'm not really anti-hippies. I just can't figure out what they want."

That provokes answers.

"My mother and father have been divorced since I was a child. He has lots of money and in place of talking to me, he just hands me money. He was mad when I wanted to make my own way out here. Says I shouldn't have to go through what he did. He doesn't realize I don't want cotton wool."

"I took my son on a camping trip. It was a lot of trouble," replied the executive from Edmonton. "He acted all the time as if he were doing it to please me and as if I were a kind of idiot."

He acknowledged that it was the first time he had, and the boy was seventeen and in some difficulty with the police before he took the trouble.

Divided in age almost equally between people under twenty-one and those of middle-age, they were determined to learn how to express themselves. The term "writing" had to cover a broad area.

And somehow you sensed in the confrontation between the groups there were answers as yet unwritten as rules.

RURAL POST OFFICES

The rural post office is a vanishing institution as postal authorities develop more and more home delivery. It may be progress, but in the country communities knotted around "hello and goodbye" crossroads, it will be missed.

Few things cut the curse of loneliness like a letter. Even impersonal circulars and magazines can help take the edge off being alone. But the country post office, located in the back section of the general store or the front room of a local house had compensations for those days when there was no mail.

Everyone had a reason for dropping in at mailtime. Old people came with fond hopes of being remembered by distant children and relatives, and remained to ease their disappointments with talk. It was a break in the days of retirement when waiting for time to pass was a poor substitute for a lifetime of activity and routine.

A letter received was a letter shared, for in such places there were no secrets. The post office was a listening post and a point of relay for information which never would reach even a local newspaper. There was gossip, a bit of rumor, facts about life, the death and birth of both man and his animals, and always the knowledge that in an emergency people would, without hesitation, make themselves available to help.

Now the postal authorities are eliminating the small mail drop places. It will be more efficient to have all mail delivered, but the efficiency is unlikely to be appreciated by those people who marked each day by a visit to the little wicket. The routine of asking, "Anything for me today?" and the invariable negative reply was always softened by the comfort of a chat about neighborhood trivialities.

In the busy city where decisions like this are taken, the rural post office appears to be an anomaly in a time of progress. But in the small places, life for many people still moves without the prompting of efficiency. The passing of this neighborhood institution will be one more sign that life grows more difficult all the time for those who know the loneliness of the twilight time.

SUMMER REWARDS

By full moon and solstice, summer began, and now the sun gently inclines to the autumn equinox. Without fanfare, nature intensifies the task of bringing to maturity the lush promises of spring.

For the countryman it is a season of work. Cultivating, weeding and haying are barely finished before the early grains demand threshing or combining. Of all, the market gardener may be the busiest, for in our compressed northern season he must plant, harvest and replant.

It is a rewarding time for the city householder to patronize the market. Wearying of fruits and vegetables that in off-

season grow jaded by long, refrigerated travel, she has the
chance to reacquaint herself with natural taste.

There is in this day and age of sterilized uniformity and
manufactured blandness nothing quite like the stinging bite of
a radish hot and fresh from the earth. Man has dried them and
frozen them and flaked them, but he still can't come near the
unique essence of new potatoes, boiled in their jackets and
dripping with butter. Not even cream and sugar can improve
a dressing of early morning dew on a plump, garden-fresh
strawberry.

Those who are wise in the ways of making the city a place
of satisfaction may be found revelling in the sights, smells and
wonderment of a summer market. Here, while night has barely
given way to day, they come to exercise their rights as share-
holders in nature's bounty, by patronizing their proxy holders,
the market gardeners.

10   *Man and His City*

Man is strangely inconsistent about his cities. He is crowding into them all over the world, creating blight spots of slums, favelas and ghettos. Suburban sprawl proliferates, while tax-hungry officials allow builders to neglect parks or to punch out trifling areas that are inadequate for any purpose. Denser and denser downtown concentrations appear with apartments and skyscrapers lacking consideration for parking, transportation or recreation areas.

While the cities grow more difficult to live in, man bewails the fact but goes on with activities that add to noise, pollution and overcrowding. August Hecksher, trying to reclaim parks in New York, suggests that modern cities are conceived as places where men live by sheer necessity, seeking their real satisfaction outside the limits. But what happens to those who can't afford to retreat to the diminishing, rural recreation areas that have survived becoming shoddy replicas of cities?

A teacher, despairing that this generation will ever be capable of making our cities fit to live in, suggests an educational campaign for city youngsters:

"Let's take them to the Expo site and let them see how man can triumph over commercial selfishness. Let's ask some of the architects, planners and builders to explain design, environment, relation of water, flowers and trees and above all show how the tyranny of trucks and cars can be avoided. Some day, members of this younger generation, driven to the extremity of reclaiming the cities for man's good, may well bless us for their experience. It's the least we can do for our children, in the face of the dreadful legacy we seem intent on leaving."

MAN AND HIS DOG

If you want a few lessons on human behavior, try watching men walking their dogs on summer evenings in the city. The summer bachelor is easily spotted. He tears along with the dog frantically trying to get in a few sniffs of familiar objects. This man has other things on his mind than simply being kind to his pet.

The man who dawdles has a problem. He pauses for the most trivial excuse in one spot, to the point where the dog may even try leading him for a change of scenery. The loiterer tries to scare up conversations with neighbors, examines the flora and fauna and spends endless time fussing. Obviously he is the victim at home of summer visitors and is trying to avoid them.

Others always seem to stare into the roadway or look up at the sky. They are avoiding confrontations with lawn and garden owners. At the least sign of a home owner moving towards the street, they will drag their charges into the roadway or else set off down the pavement at a tremendous clip.

There are questions to be asked as well. Why do so many muscular men parade tiny, yapping bits of fluff on the end of ornate leashes? Why do so many tiny men sail past hanging on for dear life as great muscular brutes of dogs appear to be taking them for an outing? The main question is, why, in the face of the old saying about a man's best friend being a dog, do so many of the evening dog walkers look so unhappy? Perhaps, dogs are really the best friends of women. The men simply carry out the walking chore!

HIGH NOON

The mythology of the American West cherishes a plot where two men build their misunderstandings until a showdown or shoot-out is inevitable. The coming confrontation of white and black in the United States has more chilling reality than myth about it, but the circumstances are much the same.

Civic authorities, their memories keen on the subject of Newark and Detroit, stockpile guns, tanks and riot control gear in astonishing amounts. Whites and blacks are buying guns over the counter. One manufacturer producing 1,500 hand guns a day is a year behind in orders.

Riot control officers and police officials are open in their recruiting of white reserves. Blacks candidly refer to the coming revolution. Tension mounts and ordinary citizens complain they are powerless to prevent the inevitable bloodshed. Congress maunders along stalled by selfish men and reactionaries.

There is sinister implication in the powerful National Rifle Association maintaining a lobby for the unrestricted sale of weapons. A black clergyman, Reverend Albert Cleage of Detroit, says, "A businessman will go anywhere — to hell, if he finds a way — for profit."

Ray Girardin, Detroit Police Commissioner, warns, "This is a revolution and people have not become aware of that. This is not just a mob or gang fight. It is the question of the survival of our cities."

Black leaders acknowledge the fact. "It is a revolution and it will be a showdown between black and white. Business goes on arming both sides. They forget this is not Nigeria or the Congo. They are going to be involved because this High Noon will be on the streets of American cities, not in a far off country."

IN NEW SUBURBIA

Suburbia is a symbol of material progress. For more and more white collar workers and even higher-paid blue collar workers, it gives evidence of prosperity, with neat lawns, outdoor barbecues, two cars and color television. It shows that the occupant is in tune with fashion and advertising. Yet, there is a worm in this rosy apple, in man's new Eden.

Social workers who felt that congestion in the old city was a cause for prejudice are surprised to find a new form in the suburbs, coming for reasons other than the traditional ones of race and religion. A fourteen-year-old boy reported he could no longer play ball for a church organized team.

"We're moving because two Italians have bought houses on our street."

He didn't question it, and when pressed said, "They'll be different than us with a lot of parties and flocks of people coming out on weekends. I guess they may be dirty, too."

His father was inclined to be angry over giving a reason, but finally admitted, "I haven't got anything against them. It's not their fault. The real estate people double-crossed us. They should know better because we have a good life with people who get along together and these people won't fit in."

Fit into what? Clergymen are keenly aware, for instance, of a changed relationship to religion. A suburbanite regards his church as a social organization used for baptism, marriage and death. They feel it has a responsibility as a factor in their children's upbringing but seldom insist on it. It is less of an emotional factor to be defended. Although conservative in outlook, modern suburban man is also aware of the increasing distaste of society for racial bias.

The prejudice arises because of a new circumstance, and part of that is lack of privacy, and strangely enough the picture window is a symbol. Speaking of them, August Hecksher in *The Human Happiness* writes:

"Too often there is nothing to see except another picture window. The important and symbolic fact about it is that it serves to let others look in, to see the things which in past civilizations have been concealed behind thick walls and in deep cavernous rooms. It is no longer true that a man's home is his castle, for a castle exists to keep other people out. The modern idea is that it is somehow morally wrong to keep others out, that privacy is a quality to be apologized for, and that intimacy is a quality to be shared, rather than to be cherished and safeguarded."

Post-1945 suburbs with patio parties, welcoming soirées and kaffee klatches led to intimacy which developed demanding inter-relationships. Some refused to be part of the homogeneity which forced on them a conformity that they found frightening, but at the root was a lack of privacy.

"I couldn't stand it," declared a computer programmer, "I know I'm supposed to be part of the frightening technological society, but, good Lord, it became a nightmare. It was nothing for my neighbor to stroll into the kitchen even when we were having company and help himself to a beer from the fridge. I don't like hockey but when I bought a color television set our living room became a Saturday night clubhouse. At that it wasn't too bad with the people we knew when we moved in, but there's two new families and they're . . . well, laugh if you want, but they're not WASPs."

He was willing to accept the demands of his social life as long as it concerned people who "fit in." He was fortunate in being able to move back to the centre of the city, and says he will miss the privacy of travel. This is another phenomenon. The commuter travels alone in his car or hides behind a newspaper on a bus or train, finding privacy between his career world and his home life with its demands.

Travel is his only privacy, and he extends this to escape from the demands of his normal life. A boat or a trailer becomes a symbol of a private life, and many will admit they use them to relieve the pressures of conformity in occupations and living as living becomes a mere extension of work. When the normal pattern of suburban inter-relationship is threatened, they can either move, or, failing that, seek more and more time away in their mobile homes on land or afloat.

The frightening aspect is the unreality of the travel. More and more people travel not for adventure or discovery but simply "to get away from it all." A Harvard study disclosed one quarter of thousands of businessmen canvassed about retirement opted for travel, but with no particular goals in mind.

North America may yet become a mobile place of people moving in their compartmentalized privacy, trying to escape the demands of shared intimacy with those who "fit in," and the unknown fear of those who "don't fit in" to the mores of suburban life.

BANKS

Imagine Stephen Leacock in a modern bank! He might mistake a trust company office for one, yield to the variety of premiums offered as enticements for depositing money and never get to meet his friendly banker.

A modern, swinging bank, however, is just the place for a touch of Leacock satire and humor. In spite of the created impression, banks still do not give away things for free. The clutter of speed boats and flower decorated sports cars in the lobby is to show the power of thrift plus the benefits of a bewildering array of savings plans.

These are elaborately encoded to colored deposit and withdrawal slips. To add to the psychedelic confusion there is an assortment of interest rates related to chequing, non-chequing and minimum balances.

What a shock this would all be to a free soul like Leacock who parlayed his relationship with an old-fashioned bank into a classic tale called "My Financial Career." Now he would have to wed a long number or suffer the wrath of the computer. It's easy to imagine him striding away, shredding colored forms and preparing to write. He would probably be mumbling the incantation, "Do Not Fold, Spindle or Mutilate!"

QUIET GARBAGE MAN

Veteran sanitary disposal officers (garbage men) must feel some of their inalienable rights are being violated. New York is seeking to buy four hundred garbage trucks designed to reduce noise and pollution odors by fifty per cent.

The police and firemen for years in Gotham have managed to upstage the sanitary employees. By loyalty to the St. Patrick's Day parade, attendance on public figures and movie stars and careful public relations, the guardians of life and property have had a more than adequate share of media exposure. This isn't confined to New York! But garbage men in almost all North American cities have cheerfully, odorously and noisily retaliated. The scrape of metal containers on a truck edge, the clattering drop to the street followed by the ringing vibration of the lid sailing over to land on the concrete brings early-morning sleepers to something like catatonic wakefulness.

They may then listen to the clattering gears on the bins, the protesting of tired transmissions and conversations conducted with full lung power. For variety there is often jolly and off-key whistling and singing. The wispy trails of more mature refuse on the street give the citizen a full measure of awareness of the men who pick up and haul away.

Put the proposal that all refuse being discarded must be placed in plastic sacks with the demand for noiseless and odorless trucks and you are taking away a set of privileges. It's bound to come before the union!

PLANNING THE CITY

Ignoring the awesome overtones of an Orwellian 1984, what kind of a world do you want in twenty years? What kind of a city do you hope for? When a group concerned about integrating adult education facilities in Metro Toronto asked Dean McCormack Smyth, of York University's continuing education school for help, he countered by suggesting they consider the objective.

His point is applicable in almost every city facing the problems of becoming a metropolis. His suggestions are all based on a desire for individuals to use themselves in more thoughtful ways and relate more intelligently to others, in order to create a dynamic human community. All of this means in effect that physical planning must be rooted in the central abilities, short-comings and needs of human beings.

Smyth asked in the first place for less political bickering and more constructive, humane leadership, including the elimination of slums and of pollution of the environment.

By 1988, the Dean wants "to know that women and girls may walk without fear of danger after dark;

" — to feel the exhilaration of Expo in a planned waterfront community;

" — to realize the air we are breathing in a Metro is not advancing the time of our death;

" — to know that tensions between the generations have been ameliorated;

" — to see emerging a higher level of inter-cultural appreciation on the part of people with Anglo-Saxon backgrounds of the cultural values of all ethnic groups;

" — to know that our systems of learning truly liberate on continuing lifelong bases people of all ages, rather than helping teenagers to prolong their juvenility and adults to rearrange their prejudices through professionalization;

" — to know that mass communications can and do contribute more to human development than to strengthening of systems of distraction organized for economic gain."

The educator stressed the fact there is a direct relationship between the character of individuals and the conditions of community life. If in turn these formal conglomerations of people called Metros are to function and become pleasant places to live in, the individuals have to be aware and perceptive. They are the ones who make the living areas habitable. Present education is inadequate because it relates to the past rather than the present or the vision of 1989.

His plea was that "we need education not only that we may acquire, but that we may share, and not only that we may act, but that we may also contemplate."

Implicit in this argument for the individual is the plea that every planning proposal be considered on the basis of how it will affect the human development of individual citizens, physically, emotionally, spiritually and financially. Any Metro in 1989 in the Dean's terms would be the result of enlightened individuals protecting their own interests as human beings rather than as imprisoned particles of financial or governmental groups.

11   *August Daze*

CLOUD WATCHING

The best show of all these days is going on against the backdrop of the August sky. Sun and clouds are holding a spectacular before the world becomes involved with the distractions of autumnal color.

Admission to this gala is free, but you are responsible for your own seating arrangements. That's easy if you remember your childhood. Select a grassy slope with a slight elevation so that you can stretch, rest and observe without getting a "crick" in your neck.

The gigantic "out of this world" screen with "living" colors will be framed by the rim of the world. The performers will dwarf even the fertile imagination of Hollywood.

Cirrus, the wispy and aloof, will perform in the upper reaches with overtones of stratospheric disdain. Stratus, the bane of airport managers, prefers to ground-hug. Nimbus is

Falstaffian, with a propensity for effects such as thunder and lightning.

No doubt Cumulus will be your favorite. On these days of quicksilver, when the sun plays hide and seek and trees turn their leaves as if blushing, the Cumulus clouds observe the "creed" of the stage. They help you, the audience, build your own dream castles in the air.

FIG LEAF FASHIONS

The fashion people are at it again. They're trying to make mini-skirts obsolescent by introducing maxi styles. The word is cover-up, but they have overlooked one point. Why not go to the limit and bring back the fig leaf?

Think of the exercise it could give those unsung heroes of the fashion battle, the copy writers. To capture the fashion dollar with fig leaf ensembles would be a real challenge for their arsenals of distorted language.

Writer Eve Merriam suggests how reasonable it all is, since there were only two consumers in the first place and each had a single, all-purpose wardrobe. Adam's was "manly, rugged with an outdoors look; Eve's was dainty, feminine, definitely slimming; accenting the fun in functional and the youth in youthful."

Sound impossible? Think of the way women have been led from hobbleskirts to mini-skirts, and of the smug assumption that they can be made to bundle up all over again, and it seems quite possible.

Picture color television, lush music and the soothing voice of the announcer saying, "See, you too can be enchanting — as glamorous as that first glittering, glamorous Eve. Tonight bedazzle the Adam in your life in your own, precious bejewelled fig leaf."

TREE HOUSE

Every boy has an inalienable right to construct and inhabit a tree house during at least one summer of his childhood. A clubhouse in the trees makes him an immediate member of that select group capable of transference to a higher mortal plane than ordinary human beings.

To be legitimate, a tree dwelling must be scrounged from materials liberated from basements, garages, construction sites and demolition operations. Genuine exotica may be found in dumps!

The site is important. The locale of the tree must be far enough away so as not to attract close parental supervision. After all, what does a mere parent know about the finer points of tree house construction? It must, however, be close enough for communication in time of danger. Bird and tree lovers often fail to grasp the significance of this kind of work.

With the inventiveness of a castaway Robinson Crusoe, the boy builder provides his shelter with a rope ladder capable of being stowed away in case of invasion by either hostile or too friendly visitors. Alone, or in selected company he will have moments of bliss in his eyrie. When rain, for instance, fails to penetrate the thatching or the wind cannot stir the structure, he can take pride in having built solidly and well.

Here in an edifice of discarded doors, dismantled packing cases, plastic windows and rusted signs, he will have his first taste of the expression, "A man's home is his castle." Growing brave, he will campaign for a night spent in his own fortress. A wise parent will allow it. The dark has a method of distorting commonplace noises into uncanny phenomena. It will take care of making a boy voluntarily terminate his abdication from a conventional home, at least at night.

TRAILER SOCIETY

From Shubenacadie to Salmon Arm, Cabot Trail to Caribou Road and St. John's to Prince George, the trailer caravans roll across Canada. They are increasing in number and come in all sizes from bunty one-wheelers, jogging behind a car, to self-contained land cruisers. They are in the tradition of nomads, who carried their homes with them as they moved.

Some observers say this tendency to wander discloses a desire to get away from conformity. Others argue it is the routine of conformity which induces people to carry the familiar carapace of their daily living as they journey from place to place.

It is of little concern to the trailer vagabonds. They go where the action happens, from Calgary Stampede to the Man and his World site to Canadian National Exhibition. Some penetrate the wilderness to find relief from pressures in simple living. As many as two hundred trailers may line up by night, waiting for morning, to be admitted to Canada's largest permanent trailer camp at Banff, Alberta.

Yet even in the carefree life there are signs of insidious influences from the workaday world which they seek to avoid. A veteran trailerman complains that the night stopovers reflect these tendencies.

"Time was," he said, "when we built a big campfire just like explorers and pioneers and sat around and sang a bit, and yarned about breakdowns and experiences, and lied a lot and made good friends. Now, at night people are too busy showing off their new gas and electric stoves and ovens, or the telescoping television antenna or the broadloom or the flush toilets, to be bothered. Trailer life isn't what it used to be. It's getting to be too much like home."

THE OTHER SIDE OF A MOUNTAIN

The Rocky Mountains are not easy to meet. They tower and glower at the plainsman and the Easterner from the crowded city or the gently rolling hills. They range sun, wind and rain around them in a daily display of dramatics with shifting curtains of mist, astounding rainbows and clouds. Sometimes they just remain passive, with the sun etching lines of prehistoric travail and struggle.

It is unbelievable for the man who sees sky as a slot in the upper reaches of canyoned streets. People who know rivers that dry up in summer heat to show muddy bottoms marvel

at the amount of water spraying from hidden, upper reaches
or spilling into shattering falls as yet untouched by meddling
engineers and developers.

They protest and marvel.

"It's so cool at night and so quiet."

Some of the two million people who pour into the Banff,
Kootenay, Yoho and Jasper parks won't believe the solace of
quiet.

"I can hear the silence at night. It bothers me."

This wilderness area, as yet resistant to exploitation and
commercialization, may yet be the refuge of Canadians and
many Americans. They may flee to it, because of sonic booms
and the constantly rising noise level of North America. But
they may also come, like twenty-year-old Therese of Three
Rivers, from curiosity.

"My parents sent me to school in France and Switzerland.
They had never been west of St. Boniface, where they went
once because an aunt of my father died. Next year I will be
married in Montreal and I was curious about Canada. Maybe
it was because my friends in Lausanne made me feel this way.
They could not believe I had never seen the mountains in
Canada. They had been there. I felt bad. So this year I come
to see for myself."

She was captivated and awed.

"They frightened me a bit. They are so big and lonely and
not like Switzerland where always there is somebody above
you. You know, like cows grazing or shepherds up above or
little places with people or skiers . . . always somebody. Here
it is different. You look up and there is just the mountain and
the very big sky . . . and I guess God."

But Therese came to terms with the mountains.

"We had a guide at Lake Louise on a horseback trip. He
had spent all his life in these mountains. I said I felt as if the
mountains would close in on me. They were so powerful and
they threatened me a bit. He just laughed and said not to
worry. Then he said, remember the mountain has two sides.

When it frightens you this way and it looks very bad, just think of the other side and the valley. There is always another side to a mountain and when it frowns on this side the sun may be tickling it on the other."

Now, she feels everyone in Canada should come and see the mountains. Europe has no rival to the Columbia ice fields.

"Touch the snow and ice and you feel it is history. Maybe this fell thousands of years ago."

There were thrills of all kinds!

"We camped at Jasper and there was a big, brown bear looking at us when we got up in the morning, and we fed a deer. We counted seven, what they called caribou, crossing the road."

If the mountains were hard to meet, they are also hard to leave.

"We saw Athabaska Falls and Maligne Canyon and I made pictures to send to Europe. I wanted to pick what they call devil's paint brushes and Arctic poppies, but they said it was illegal. When we are married, I will bring my husband here because he is an artist, at least for a hobby. He must paint the lake called Peyto. This is the strangest color I have ever seen."

Did she feel at home in this part of Canada which was strange to her?

"Oh yes. I see the flags and the Centennial symbols but I wonder sometimes why there seem to be so many Americans. But I guess they come because they like it."

Did anyone make her feel strange because she was French-speaking?

"I found some people from Quebec and they were like myself, excited," she laughed. "And only once when I spoke French did a man start to argue about the French badges on the people's uniforms who work in the parks. I just said it made me feel good to know Canada was both French and English and when he seemed to get a little angry I just said it didn't bother me because I knew there were two sides for every mountain. He just shrugged his shoulders and went away."

AUGUST REVERIE

There is a bitter-sweet touch in the coolness of the night breath of the fulfilling month of August. The vacationer feels it when the quiet air by the still water smells of fires lit to "take the chill off" summer dwellings.

The pulse of growth yields to the process of ripening. For the countryman it is the season of harvest. Even the word "ripe" is a derivation of "reap." "Plenty" dates to the Latin source "full." The mystical bond of man and land is now approaching the maturity of full partnership that began on spring days with the marriage of seed and soil.

The transplanted city dweller can be forgiven for finding sadness. He senses the forthcoming loss of holiday freedom. In an even more significant way the man of urban streets and complexities envies those who still live and work in harmony with nature.

The holidayer has echoes of pioneer ancestors stirring his heart and blood, and the refrain of their siren song tells of an uncomplicated existence. He savors it for the moment, aware that it will be silenced by a practical daylight. Yet now he earnestly wishes in this tranquil time for magic or mystery, powerful enough to vanquish the tyranny of duty and the habits of an existence which, while giving more and more tangible evidence of material progress, bestow less and less of the intangibles of inner satisfaction.

HURRYING TIME

Benjamin Franklin was concerned that men should not squander time because, "it is the stuff life is made of." He would have been shocked by the way we hurry it along. Time may be our most precious commodity, but we seem determined to give concern to the future at the expense of the present.

We're assailed by admonitions of what is to come. Every school child knows a sinking feeling when the enjoyment of August is overshadowed by the sight of schoolbooks and supplies in every class of store from corner confectionery or pharmacy to supermarket.

The seasonal display of fashions for women always defied logic. Furs are shown in midsummer and bikinis in deepest winter. Now men's haberdashers are employing similar tactics. It's disconcerting to be told on a blazing day that we must buy overcoats of a certain color and style or be definitely out of the fashion swim.

Poor old Santa Claus must be the most confused character of all, because of our propensity for advancing the Christmas buying season. No wonder he makes mistakes on Christmas Eve. Since he must show himself in so many shopping plazas in snowless fall, he has become more used to airplane controls than reindeer reins.

To cap the whole matter of hurrying time, we urge men to retire early and then give them ticking watches as remembrances. The moral seems to be that man must be reminded at all times of the need to stop hurrying time.

COOL SPELL

Here in the northern latitudes, where summers are limited, we take full advantage of July heat and sun. Flaming sunburns attest to cases of desire outweighing reason. In spite of the summer addiction, however, we still welcome an occasional cool spell.

A summer rain and moderate weather take the pulsing heat from the stone and concrete of the city. Throbbing machines are relieved of making artificial coolness. An added cover gives comfort as we snuggle into deep sleep.

The countryman finds energy for tasks he postponed because of the heat. The camper stokes his fire and is glad of the warmth. Vacationers are bundled up as they walk in curiously quiet resorts. Cottagers sense a touch of pioneering spirit as they cut and haul wood for evening sessions by roaring fireplaces. Lakes are stilled. There are no nocturnal swimmers or noisy boat enthusiasts. You can once again hear the call of the whippoorwill and the loon. The sun and heat will return, but the temporary coolness is a welcome respite.

TURNING POINT

The August moon, the last full one of summer, extravagantly colored blood red and golden yellow, was a symbol. It seemed to adopt the color of the roadside surf of goldenrod and the brilliant crimson slashes of sumac to warn that summer is at last on the turn.

Mornings come in mistily, and the world is simply in less of a hurry. Wild, green grapes drape on abandoned fences waiting for frost to enrol them in the royal purple. Roadside stands blaze with the contrasting colors of fruit and vegetables designed to attract returning vacationers to stop and tarry.

The cycle of summer edges with a new purpose. Acorns and nuts mellow and ripen in anticipation of the demand by those inveterate hoarders, the squirrels and chipmunks. The milkweed waits with pregnant pods for the opportune time to rupture and let the September breeze carry its seed and individual parachutes on a campaign of propagation.

Blackbirds are gossipy. Migrating birds are nervously looking for departing signals while children studiously avoid the heavily-accented significance of "Back to School" sales. Our only bonus is the slower pace. It indicates that nature enjoys dawdling before entering Autumn, the finale of the phenomenon of growth which began deep in the heart of the soil, while we were still gripped by the outward evidence of winter.

A SUMMER FEAST

Jacques Cartier saw fields of maize growing on what is now Montreal. This forerunner of today's corn originated in South America, probably Guatemala. The early explorers marvelled at how the Indians had developed it as a food staple over such vast areas of the Americas.

We are the beneficiaries. Fortunate gardeners may peel back the green sheaths and the browned tassels and convey the corn directly to the pot of boiling, fresh water. Then the steaming, golden cobs are served.

Here is ambrosia, as the butter melts, flowing down the ridges of kernels, ready to anoint a waiting chin. Each kernel explodes with its own content of flavor. Small boys may be overcome by valiant efforts to pile up stripped cobs as numerical tributes to gustatory appreciation. A father will be forgiven for aiding the cause by surreptitiously contributing a few illegal cobs.

The taste of "corn on the cob" is a genuine New World sensation. Just as the required time between stalk and pot is fleeting, so also is the length of the season, because a hot August sun soon matures the crop.

May your summer table be graced by "corn on the cob." While enjoying it may you be grateful to the originators — the Indians. We are often inclined to forget that our first citizens did leave more by way of legacies than simply that of being consistent losers in TV westerns.

A TOUCH OF SADNESS

The cottager feels it as he carries fire logs, now an evening necessity and no longer a summer affectation. The evening sky is extravagantly colored but the lake water is black. On the surface there are brown and wilted leaves, like gentle hints from nature.

The countryman senses it in the shrilling of the crickets in the evening. He sees ascending plumes of smoke in the crisp, morning air from the chimneys of neighboring farm homes. His cows have moved up of their own accord from the pastures, to indicate that they wouldn't mind stabling on chilly nights.

The city shopper at farm markets has a choice of a full variety of produce. Potatoes are no longer labelled as new. Ruddy-cheeked saleswomen suggest with a touch of warning that now is the time to pickle and preserve, because fall is coming.

Parents point silently to a diminishing August when problems of discipline come up in the family. Elders sit for long hours in the sun as if hoping to store the warmth for reserve.

The color and spectacle of autumn lies ahead, but we are all subtly sad because the robust days of summer heat and holiday are on the wane.

CRICKET TIME

The final days of August have an edge of melancholy for a summer vacationer. Crowds at many resorts are diminished by people unwilling to get involved in the Russian roulette of Labor Day weekend traffic.

Boxes and cartons on a cottage verandah are evidence of feminine concern for decampment. Children are defensively boisterous or remain morose in the face of a new school term.

Man is vaguely troubled when he comes awake in the night to the sound of gently lapping waters and rustling leaves. He thinks of traffic and noise, routines of work and home and the discipline of clock time, and wishes he could simply stop the world.

Then, as if adding insult to injury, he hears the crickets. Their sound is the symbol of passing summer, a full beat now, which will slow down and finally stop as autumn passes. The night fiddlers, all male, are frantically seeking mates in a brief span of time, a reminder of the inexorable cycles which guide all the creatures of earth.

The crickets add a bitter-sweet reminder to the dwindling days of a man's vacation freedom.

12 *September Song*

SEPTEMBER

In France they used to describe September as the May of autumn. Ninth month in our calendar, it was seventh for the Romans and retained the name. The actual changeover was in 1752 when the English moved the beginning of the year from March to January.

The Saxons, harvesting their main crop, called it Barley Month. We know it as a time when the birches yellow and we're cheered by the blue of gentian. Nights refresh with coolness and the days are seldom uncomfortably hot.

The urgency of summer slows down for the maturing process of autumn. Sumacs splash scarlet plumage, indicating that the time of chlorophyll and growth is past.

Although September can be fickle and chilly, we expect and hope for a month of golden warmth as a prelude to the full pageant of autumn.

COUNTRY STORES

Down the dusty roads that spread vein-like away from the highways of Ontario and Quebec, the motorist will find interesting discoveries. For instance, there still exist at crossroads and in the heart of rural valleys, country stores which remain unchanged, at least in essence.

Gasoline pumps and oil racks have taken over from hitching posts and watering troughs. Old signs and new signs spatter the outside walls in picturesque disorganization. Some remain to advertise products which have even vanished from the shelves.

Window displays are not a factor of merchandising. Shoppers here come for specific purposes in place of browsing. The owner, a rugged individualist, will tell you proudly he is a "general merchant."

In this quiet place of oiled floors and the mingled aroma of everything from spices to molasses, from harness oil to dried codfish, the visitor glimpses traces of the unhurried past.

The country stores of our area exist because they are integral parts of communities as yet undisturbed by the demands of highways and expanding cities. No one can predict how long they will survive, so they are now to be cherished as restful spots where good conversation takes precedence over commerce.

COUNTRY KITCHENS

Country kitchens are places of sheer delight in September. Sunlight filters through windows clustered with ivy and flowering plants to dapple the piles of garden produce. The scents, smells and sounds prove that the art of canning, pickling and preserving is not completely lost.

The spicy scent betrays tomatoes bubbling in kettles and being transformed into chili sauce. Sunlight makes jewels of corn kernels speckled with flecks of green and of red pepper in jars, labelled "Corn Relish — 69" with a loving care rivalling a vintner's pride in a vintage year. Slim, green gherkins bob in a secret preservative solution, whose mystery was inherited or perfected by the lady of the household as carefully as those of the clerical liqueur makers of Europe.

It is the time when baskets of fruit and vegetables may even be crowded into tiny, apartment kitchens. It is harvest time and most women respond instinctively to preparation for the bleak season of winter. They pridefully know that none of man's devices and processes for mass preservation of produce of the harvest can really touch the simple one that includes a woman's benediction.

On a blustery day, when winter seems permanent, they will be rewarded by family and husbandly response to a jar of home pickles or preserves. It will have in it the subtle essence of sunlight, full harvest flavor and the satisfaction of a September kitchen.

FLOWERS OF SEPTEMBER

There is royal pageantry in the way flowers show up before autumn converts the landscape into a thing of browns and golds. Suddenly we are aware of the massed brilliance and psychedelic color spilling and frothing from the disorder of roadsides to the geometric precision of park borders.

Perhaps the asters, petunias, geraniums and begonias were there all the time and we were too busy to pay attention. Has the first gentle pruning of leaves and foliage brought the flowers into our vision?

In any case, whether cultivated or growing in forgotten plots as legacies of former care, the flowers of September are in full and mature splendor. Here and there a maple shows a flash of red, while climbing vines on old walls are tinged in deep scarlet, but we scarcely notice. For the moment, the frothing color of the flowers is truly the attention-getter.

UNCHANGING NATURE

This is the golden time of harvest. Grain fields splotch the countryside. Even the stubble of early cutting has a yellowish afterglow that contrasts with the green hedges, trees and pasture.

The sight of farmers of the sects such as Amish and Mennonite harvesting with old-fashioned implements is almost a shock. These scenes, reminiscent of the pioneers, contrast sharply with the working of intricate machinery power, operated for speed and labor-saving on neighboring farms.

The sturdy men who resist change seem to be almost an anomaly in this day of dedication to the machine. Yet, for all of the ingenuity of man, the way of nature remains constant. The growth of seed in a plot scratched by primitive implements or cultivated by monster machines is the same. It requires soil fertility, moisture and sun to achieve the maturity of harvest.

For all men, whether they work with the methods of their forefathers or plan for atomic powered implements, the satisfaction is the same, for a bountiful harvest is bestowed in the ageless cycle and manner of nature.

SEPTEMBER THE GOLDEN

Quiet and solitude, so rare in these days of congestion and noise, bring wonderful compensation in golden September. Every human should make the effort to cast off the stridencies and the cares of the busy places and seek out secluded spots.

Find a clump of unspoiled pines or cedars where the breeze whispers softly. Search for a stream, untouched by polluting carelessness, and listen to the way it chides the tickling stones. A deserted stone wall, monument to pioneer effort, will give you a vine-cushioned backing for an immersion in the warmth of the September sun.

Then take the advice of J. B. Priestley, who himself enjoys the unspoiled pleasures of an Isle of Wight retreat, as a guide to solitary satisfaction:

"Any man can be fussy and rid himself of energy all over the place, but a man has to have something in himself before he can settle down to do nothing. He must have reserves to draw upon, must be able to plunge into strange, slow rivers of dream and reverie, must at heart be a poet."

BIOLOGICAL TIME CLOCK

Man seemingly can't fool nature. He's pushing the speed barriers back, and he can flit around the world and literally arrive back before he started in terms of time zones, but he can't fool his biological time clock. It's a built-in check, and the businessman who tries to defy the time zones will find himself up against jet fatigue.

According to Dr. Freund of the American aviation authority, it isn't the distance. You can fly north and south to your heart's delight if you stay in the same time zone. Throw the time sequence off and you put your system out of kilter. A person will be sleeping and eating when he shouldn't be.

Airlines naturally are not prone to stress these factors, but organizations such as the Ontario Trade and Development Board recognize it. They take parties of businessmen overseas on a Friday to allow a weekend of rest before Monday appointments.

Critics say supersonic flight will complicate the matter to the point where long distance travellers will need a week of rest at each end of their junket. Airlines suggest passengers on SST can fly overseas and return in the same day, making their appointments in such a way as to stay within their Circadian rhythms. That's what regulates metabolism, energy periods, rest, pulse and body functions.

Pilots express concern about the effect of supersonic flights. Everyone agrees, however, on the need for rest after prolonged flight through time zones. The layman may well wonder where the advantage is in speed over more leisurely travel if you have to rest at your destination.

An example of precaution against jet fatigue happened when Aleksei Kosygin arrived in New York from Moscow. It was a full week before he faced a press conference. The Soviet Premier was obviously repairing his biological time clock.

WATCHING

September is ideal for practising the art of watching. Reaction comes naturally as the trees rust into autumnal color. The screen of leaf and foliage is thinning in a subtle strip tease, creating new vistas.

The squirrels are frenetically flitting around. Tiny birds in overwhelming numbers feast on ripe seeds. Starlings shiver the air in morning and evening flights to harvest fields. Crows bicker over territorial rights and jays scold everyone on general principles.

This is a month when teachers should obey impulse, disregard rigidities and convene classes in the nearest field, forest or park. Thucydides, the population figures for Brasilia, or the history of the Suez Canal may be sacrificed, but will it really matter?

S. I. Hayakawa, the semanticist, suggests that the alienation of the young may be caused by television. There is no interaction possible with an electronic baby-sitter.

An expedition in the musky glory of September qualifies in developing environmental awareness. It may even help to put "Hogan's Heroes" or "Garrison's Gorillas" into perspective.

AN OFT-FORGOTTEN POINT

In all the interest shown in communications, one point is often forgotten. Simple communication is a basis of life. The cry of the baby is the beginning. The audible sound sets off communication in all forms, until the last gasp signals the departure of life.

"You have a son!"

Doctor to father, who immediately uses the telephone and telegraph to convey information! The type in the newspaper column and the handwriting in personal notes show concrete forms of communication.

The child learns to sense forms and shapes, and feels the tactility of everything from crib bars to the flesh of his mother and the hands of nurses. Sounds add to all the other sensory information already stored in the memory bank, presumably beginning in the womb. Heat and cold. Shapes, sounds, dimensions and even the crying which the youngster learns to use as a signal of will, even of blackmail.

Think of the conscious facts of memory regarding the growing up process. The shadows in a darkened room, the sounds of the house and the tiny sounds coming into focus when a night-stilled world quenches the normal ones. The ominous note of a squeaky floor or the happiness of a chirrupy bird. Flickering light or the mystery of night and day.

Sizes? The dimension of a soft creature that rubbed against your legs and of a parent looming over you saying "C.A.T."

"Good."

They gave you a sense of warmth and comfort in this word. It seemed to please them, and they touched you gently or smoothed your arm with their fingertips.

"Bad."

They frowned. They seemed angry. This was harsh. They tapped you or even pinched and gave you pain when they spoke.

One of my first conscious memories was of losing a brightly colored, wooden pull toy down an abandoned cellarway. There were a number of lessons about this. The board gave way and the toy fell in. I was frightened and moved away. I could look down in the blackness and make out the form of the toy. I had been warned by gestures and instruction to stay away from the place. In admitting that I had lost the toy, I had to admit my guilt.

But this is only the beginning of the effects of communication on our lives. There's the non-verbalizing between playmates before they learn to speak. The relationships at school and the emergence of a vocabulary.

The development of clandestine communication in a school between youngsters to avoid discipline and teacher notice.

Think of the association of ideas! A friend was literally

carried to church as a youngster because of his terror. It was a lofty old edifice and the sight of the preacher, who had a resonant voice, perched up in the pulpit, made him think of vultures. Somewhere he had come in contact with both information and misinformation about vultures, and when he first looked at that pulpit his imaginings seemed to come true. His parents, who felt his terror was some form of godlessness, insisted on dragging him to church, and he feels, rightly or wrongly, that many of his hangups in later life came about because of this experience.

Each new step in the child's development is somehow associated with communicating. Adolescence and travel. Think of the child who makes a trip alone by train or plane to visit a relative. Learning about strangers and how each individual wraps himself in a personal form of isolation, and knowing how easy it is to penetrate with some and how others resent any interference.

The influence of school, university and a career. The inability of some teachers to share and participate in the learning process and the ease with which others do so. Relationships and romance, real or imagined?

How to make contact with a new employer, or even the hiring officer? Talking to other members of the firm. To explain work to a wife and to begin communications with a child of your own. Social life, political life, community life, business life — each demands communication.

All through life and in retirement there are new demands. Will a man or woman make new contacts for adjustment, activate new portions of their minds to cope with inactivity? The communication of anxieties or pain symptoms to a doctor.

Even after death the routine of the telephone and telegraph and notice in print comes into operation. Now there may be a continuing form of communication by way of sound tape or film for certain people, so that there is a more active communications memory than simply a tombstone. It's one approach for considering communications and man!

THE MISTS OF AUTUMN

On fall mornings when the city discloses signs of foggy murkiness, you can be assured the country is bathed in the mists of autumn. Night chill, like a premonition of winter, reacts to the earth which still holds the warmth of day. Through the night the frothy reaction packs up, filling the environment like a massive, fallen cloud.

In the early morning, before the sun musters enough strength to dissipate the filmy stuff, there is a mysterious effect throughout the countryside. Distances are distorted. A tree, a fence or a landmark looms up suddenly, taking the walker by surprise. Slowly moving cars stretch beams of light like feelers down country roads.

Far away noises have amazing clarity. A diesel honks hoarsely and continuously with the impatience of a liner threading a sea filled with icebergs. Snatches of conversation may be heard momentarily and distinctly only to fade like short wave radio reception. Tinkling cow bells indicate the impatience of the wearers with a delay in their milking time.

Then comes the magic of sunlight and warmth. The pearly grey mist glints and shimmers and begins to part, revealing vistas of trees in their ceremonial colors. Headlands and green slopes unfold and buildings appear in proper dimension. Checkered squares of brown cultivated earth contrast with the vivid green ones of fall seeding.

The lowlands, the marshes and the deeper valley are the stubborn ones, and remain shrouded for a time. Man moves to his work. The tiny creatures and insects revive from their temporary dormancy and enjoy the reprieve. Autumn mists are another example of man's seasonal bounty in the way of spectacle and mystery.

THE EQUINOXES

The mystery of the equinoxes has given rise to many speculations about their significance. Great storms and promised

storms rage or merely threaten in the equatorial latitudes. Yet
the equinoxes are merely part of the celestial calendar, and
while they do not in actual fact correspond to the opening of
the spring and fall seasons, they give us reason for hope.

The vernal equinox of March holds promise of spring relief
from bleak weather. The autumnal equinox of September is
a symbol for fall's pageant of color and harvest glory.

Between the twenty-first and twenty-third of September a
day and a night are equal. The twenty-four hours become
divided into identical segments of twelve. The sun ascends for
six hours and descends for six hours.

Twice a year we share this phenomenon, which is a constant
occurrence for those who live on the equator. This is a matter
of the pull of gravity of sun and moon on the bulging equatorial protuberance of the spheroid which is earth.

It may shock some to hear that our earth is not a smooth
sphere. Can it be possible that those turbulences with girls'
names represent a violent feminine reaction to the bulging
midriff? It may not be logical, but almost any man will be
bound to admit it is a possibility.

CRICKETS

Rabelais thought people should be as merry as crickets. He
may have been referring to humans or crickets when he said,
"Above the pitch, out of tune and off the hinges."

There is something incongruous about these insects with
their peculiar equipment for jumping and noisemaking. The
shrilling "song" comes from rubbing the toothed ridge of the
back wings on a drumskin-like portion of the front wings.

Man has always cherished crickets. Eastern society makes
household possessions of them in ornate cages, as omens of
good fortune and cheer. Here, on warm summer evenings,
country residents and visitors glory in their full sound, which
if not tuneful is at least comfortably seasonal and happy. When
the chill of fall is being repulsed by a blaze in the fireplace,

the trilling "cheerrupp" of a guest cricket evokes pleasant memories of Charles Dickens.

Yet, in the final analysis, man may treasure his deepest feeling towards crickets because it is a species of Nature's creation where the female remains silent.

FIRST FALL RAINS

The first rains of fall are housekeeping ones in the city. The lawns were dry, the flowers trying desperately to keep their vividness and the streets grey and littered. Nature decided to clean the place up before the real showing of colors.

With the equinox as a reasonable excuse, the sluicing rain, after a few gentle, pattering warnings, came pouring down. It plucked dead leaves from the trees and bushes and sent them merrily down into the brimming gutters. Grass assumed a green rivalling spring brilliance. Flowers lifted tiring heads. Grey concrete almost gleamed.

The city dweller gloried in rain-washed air and moved about in the mistiness, savoring the rediscovered fresh scent of earth. Car tires whispered and children splashed in puddles with an abandonment worthy of a warm April.

Then the rain came back. This time it was gentle, nudging reluctant debris snagged behind miniature dikes. It nibbled down windows and caressed cheeks. It fairly whispered in the ears of anyone who would listen, "The big snow is coming, so please get ready."

FALL

It's difficult to keep from rhapsodizing when fall comes quietly to the landscape. Soft and warm days alternate with cool nights cushioned in the dawn hours by fog and mist veils.

Modern man, who seems preoccupied by buildings, briefly rediscovers the outdoors. He haunts parks, lingers on sidewalks, drives in the countryside and reminisces about the hills and fields of his childhood.

Fall is the season that bestows the power of voicing on the trees. The leaves rustle, whisper and lisp at the urging of every breeze and air movement. Nature is being kind in allowing them expression before they are plucked from the limbs and branches by the relentless power of the late season rain and wind.

In fall there is very little questioning of their identity by Canadians. The question is somehow irrelevant during this season of total environmental glory.

THE CALENDAR

In a way man recognizes the full and spicy autumn as the finale of the year. Harvest and color serve as a final curtain for the natural cycle which began with the warmth and fertility of spring.

The ancient Romans had ten variable months in the year, and when reformers tried to pin a twelve month calendar to what Shakespeare later called "the inconstant moon," their year was ten days shy of the total racked up by the sun. In a rare display of "amateur fixing" they inserted an elastic month to make up the shortage every second year. They never quite matched the vagaries of the sun, and birthday calculations would have taxed a modern computer.

Julius Caesar took over the yearly deficit of sixty-odd days and pushed in two extra months to try to cope with another factor, the vernal equinox. Thus, the Julian calendar began a complicated tenure on January 1, 46 B.C.

Pope Gregory XIII decided to stop the finagling, but he still had a shortage to make up of over a week of time before his schedule took over as a calendar in 1582 A.D. Aware of the basic problem of natural phenomena making new rules for differing circumstances, he took a precaution. The double zero century year must not be a leap year unless it can be divided evenly by 400. So don't count on a leap year in 2100!

The Gregorian year is some twenty-seven seconds too long,

and reformers would love to stabilize it. They want thirteen equal months of twenty-eight days each and one day as a special holiday, probably honoring calendar makers. Days and dates of the year would remain constant.

John Ciardi, the American poet once suggested we readopt the Hebraic calendar. He said the Jews, with more time than the Romans to learn themselves by heart, had the good sense to choose September as the year's end. In these bronzed days of September the idea makes sense to any man's heart.

13   *To Walk in October*

DARKNESS

Fall is a time when we rediscover the infinite variety of darkness. Dusk is neither a time of gathering gloom nor a fast shutter of night. It is instead a varied program of grey, black and silver clouds, often spectacularly backlighted by the molten lava effects of the vanishing sun.

The approach of evening may give rosy tips to the hills, while the valleys seem spattered with fragments of black and silver. A spire stands in golden illumination above the dark bulk of the church. Rivers are black in the folds of the hills, only to broaden around a turn into shining platters.

Flocks of birds move from darkening stubble into the sky and become quivering clouds of bright fragments in the shafts of light. A countryman moving from place to place with his chores alternates from light to shadow and back again.

Old men study the effects of cloud and sun, as if seeking

signs and omens. They appear to draw satisfaction from the scene and, being constrained to make observations, comment sagely, if not uniquely, on the shortening of the days of October.

SOUNDS OF NIGHT

Sounds are a compensation for night in the country. Even on the darkest occasion of summer and early fall there is companionship and comfort in the audible presence of birds and insects.

The songs of the birds dwindle by late summer, and the rustling, whispering and buzzing of the insects take over.

Then come the chilling nights when the thermometer teeters on the edge of freezing point. There is an eerie silence outside. Inside, in woodsheds and kitchens, a venturesome cricket is welcomed.

The relaxing warmth of a brief Indian summer will rejuvenate a diminished orchestra by night. It is only temporary, because the first deep frost will produce the night silence of autumn.

This is a quiet broken only by isolated sounds. Boots clump on stiffened ground. Foxes yelp on distant hills. There is a melancholy overtone in the hoot of an owl on a lonely vigil. The countryside is preparing for the quiet sleep of winter.

CATS

Cats are haughty creatures. They manage to achieve a great deal of human care and affection without reciprocation. Pampering seems to be a prerogative rather than a bestowed favor.

Country cats are also wily. As the nights grow chillier, they forsake nocturnal prowling and scheme to be admitted to the house. They are accomplished at subterfuge. An apparently slumbering cat by a doorstep will bolt at tremendous speed through a partially opened door.

At milking time, even the surliest cat will display an external appearance of goodwill. But the imperious dignity will not be lowered one whit. Even while being challenged in the house, or tossed out, a cat may indulge in a bit of fawning or leg-rubbing, but never as a supplicant.

The late Peter McArthur felt that cats were like politicians. He said that cats had fine, purring manners, sharp and concealed claws, and, politically, were good mousers. They also knew how to keep themselves easy in public office.

Peter, like many other people, recognized their usefulness and overlooked their superior ways and desire for cosiness. He even raised no objection to their petty grafting at milking time.

THINGS!

"I am not concerned about man running out of space for people," complained the returning vacationer, "but I am worried that he is not going to find room for his stuff. In North America, the things we own and keep on buying will bury us."

The suburbanite was trying to store his trailer for the winter. He bought it to compensate for the usual cottage vacation, abandoned because of weekend travel difficulties in and out of the city. It had been supplemented with a power cruiser and trailer.

The backyard was out, because of an elaborate barbecue and swimming pool and summer furniture.

His recreation room is filled with a billiard table. This was to be a centre of indoor recreation on rainy days, but his son and daughter even lost interest in the hi-fi set, preferring to strum guitars and compose protest songs about materialism and affluence.

The suburban garage is filled with a power-mower, a snow blower, a ski-doo and his wife's small car. The driveway is occupied by his own car and an older car purchased for a daughter who decided she needed transportation to and from meetings of her college revolt group.

"We are contemplating," he said gloomily, "renting space in a trailer park and leaving our home for storing things in. Do you know, when my doctor prescribed an exercise machine for overweight, the only place I could find for it was in the living room. Even the kitchen is overcrowded since we bought the dishwasher."

OCTOBER

October is a month of spicy contentment. The air is perfumed and winey. The landscape is vivid with colorations that grow more intense from day to day.

It is a time of activity, when squirrels flicker about and birds move like animated splotches against the sky. Dogs race about on never-ending forays. Children play with exuberance, as if trying to defeat the earlier dusk.

Leaves, early fallen, seem to shift about in expectation of November winds. Even in the orchards, apples forsake their clinging and plop into the grass.

A countryman moves with an October fever. It is a time for striding across stubble fields to admire fat pumpkins and squash nestling in drying vines. This is the month for admiring scarlet creepers or a golden row of maples reflected in the darkened waters of a pond. It is October, without winter bleakness or April urgency. It has an ample warmth without summer discomfort. October fever is satisfying!

PUMPKIN PIE

The great, orange jewels of the vegetable kingdom are scattered throughout the countryside in fall profusion. They gleam in piles by roadside kiosks, stand stacked on far verandahs and leer with gap-toothed artistry from schoolhouse windows in anticipation of Hallowe'en frolic.

Pumpkins belong to the season of autumn. No harvest festival or simulated horn of plenty would be complete without the ridged, orange spheres that grow in such profusion without lavish care. Farmers who would ordinarily shun the "woman's work" of vegetable growing have no compunction in spring scattering of the large, flat seeds.

Fall-stimulated appetites deserve pumpkin pie. Made spicy

with cinnamon, ginger and nutmeg and even an adventurous dash of cloves, a pumpkin pie in the baking scents a kitchen with memories. Reward yourself with one and you'll agree with John Greenleaf Whittier when he said that nothing recreated the past like good, rich pumpkin pie.

A REAL FIREPLACE

We live in a world of simulation and imitation. The sign in the department store window proclaims the product on the mannequin to be a "Genuine Fake Fur Coat." The furniture salesman points proudly to the chrome-like edging on a kitchen table and says, "That's actually plastic but no one will be able to tell it from chrome-stripping."

Man wears synthetic fibres in place of cotton or wool. He accepts artificial sweetness in place of sugar in an attempt to lose weight. Most of his prepared food has some form of substitution for natural ingredients. By now he has given up trying to tell real flowers from the constructed ones in salons and cafes.

Somehow the average man, who was usually so keen about avoiding sham, has given up fighting the trend. Yet there is one place where he draws the line. Ask any real estate man and he'll tell you that while a wife on a house inspection will search out the cupboard and storage space, the man heads for the living room. Then, while looking at the fireplace, he'll demand, "is it a real one?" in a tone suggesting that he will not settle for anything else.

On nippy fall nights we can be pleased that man's compromise for substitution is not a total abdication of the real.

BURNING THE LEAVES

Man is a perplexing creature. He seems unable to control the processes which pour tons of industrial noxious residue into the air from smokestacks. On the other hand, he is most diligent in preventing his neighbor from the simple task of burning autumn leaves in an urban area.

This is one time when the countryman or the small town resident has the advantage. Unhindered by regulation or by-law and secure in the knowledge that he is not posing a fire hazard he allows himself the pleasure of at least a token leaf burning each November.

It is an emotional rite and a happy one, for leaf smoke is truly the incense of brown Fall. He stands like the ceremonial priest of an ancient ritual, a mysterious figure in the grey veils of smoke, and remembers other autumns and the glorious scents. It may be a memory of the spiciness of late pickling in a warm kitchen, the almost forgotten smell of drying apples on their racks or the frothy tanginess of fresh-pressed cider. The yen for roasting chestnuts may be almost overpowering.

Perhaps it's just as well that burning leaves is forbidden in the cities. People from similar backgrounds, now transplanted to the rigidity of city ways, might not be able to stand the effects of such a leaf smoke-induced "trip."

HUNTER'S MOON

The full moon of October is the moon of the hunter. Long before the mechanical wizardry of meteorology, old men scanned the full face of it, trying to discern evidence of what winter held in store.

Young men followed baying dogs across new-frozen fields in search of game. Wily coons used the inherited instincts accumulated from the time when man, emerging as a species, first became a predator in place of a neighbor.

Today an October moon, wreathed in icy mist or suffused by shades of orange, is more liable to inspire a song than a prognosis. Game has probably been depleted or dispersed by advancing urbanization.

Yet the hunter's moon can evoke mysterious feelings in us. Man has walked on it, but we still cherish the mystery of the moon. May we still wonder at the possibility of its being able to invoke some winter revenge on man, in retaliation for its own loss of remote privacy.

FALLING LEAVES

The landscape is being feathered by falling leaves. Rains and vagrant breezes pluck colored patches from the banner of foliage on the trees and send them fluttering earthwards.

Released, they are playthings for children and wind. Tidy gardeners rake them into neat piles where they are magnets for children anxious to send them flying once again in all directions.

The wind is a prankster of many kinds where the homeless leaves are concerned. Tiny breezes tug at them nervously. Stronger ones send them skittering along paths and roads. Gusts whirl them about in giddy games. Zephyrs pluck them about and plaster them into hedgerows. A full October gale bundles the colored fragments into heaps against buildings and obstructions. Pelting rain and blowing wind combine at times, as if anxious to get on with the autumnal denuding in preparation for winter.

On quiet days the fallen leaves are mere mementoes of spring and summer growth and bloom. Then, on a bright and windy day when someone whispers "Indian summer" in a tone of awe, there will be that first real bonfire of the leaves. The air will be perfumed with the incense and we will be touched with the bitter-sweet feeling of the final benediction of autumn.

THE JOYS OF WALKING

While a few stubborn ones remain on the trees to glisten and sparkle as the sun glints on the morning frost, there are still enough leaves on the ground to provide a rustling sensation. This is the time to rediscover the glory of walking. In an age when vehicles have tyrannized us with ease and comfort, there is pure joy in rediscovering our legs as a natural means of locomotion.

In the fall season the setting can be parkland, a quiet street, or a country road. The virtue of walking has been hailed for centuries by contemplative people. It was pointed out that men should be like camels, the only known beasts to ruminate while walking. A visitor calling on Wordsworth was told by the servant, "Here is his library but his study is outdoors."

Re-read the essay on walking by Thoreau, and thus be prepared for the experience of walking in the bountiful days of late fall. He relates, for instance:

"We had a remarkable sunset one day last November. I was walking in a meadow, the source of a small brook, when the sun at last, just before setting, after a cold gray day, reached a clear stratum in the horizon and the softest, brightest morning sunlight fell on the dry grass and on the stems of the trees in the opposite horizon and on the leaves of the shrub oaks on the hillside, while our shadows stretched long over the meadow eastward, as if we were the only motes in its beams. It was such a light as we could not have imagined a moment before, and the air also was so warm and serene that nothing was wanting to make a paradise of that meadow. When we reflected that this was not a solitary phenomenon, never to happen again, but that it would happen forever and ever, an infinite number of evenings, and cheer and reassure the latest child that walked there, it was more glorious still."

It is a long time since Thoreau lived by Walden Pond, but there are still rewards in nature in spite of progress. Yet the fact remains that for the most satisfactory walking we must get away from the evidence of man's conquest of nature.

Perspective returns in walking. Quiet farm houses with windows like friendly eyes glow at you. Stone fences with vivid, clinging vines and aged posts and rails that wear the patina of time make you remember. Forgotten lines come back to mind such as those by C. T. Davis once memorized for the rote of school:

> "Who walks a road with love will never walk
> That road alone again.
> Old lonely things will garb them in the guise
> Of beauty glowing with remembered eyes."

A park shielded from the sounds and distractions of commerce is rare blessing in a city. It influences those who come to sit and read, or sit and think, or simply to sit and stare. It resounds to children, their cries the true signals of one liberated from the constricting confinement of apartments and streets monopolized by vehicular traffic.

If only town planners and civic officials could be made to walk around the city in the winey air of fall. There is a distinct impression that they scan the landscape and environment through the shifting windows of cars and cabs and then go back to plan more ways of confining the human spirit. Make them sample a park in the fall and surely commonsense and reality would govern the next decision between development interest as opposed to individual liberation.

No man walks alone these bright days. Memory always walks along. The writers and poets knew this, as witness Hilaire Belloc:

> "The great hills of the South Country
> They stand along the sea;
> And it's there walking in the high woods
> That I could wish to be,
> And the men that were boys when I was a boy
> Walking along with me."

There may be a touch of sadness if you read Thoreau before walking. He quotes Sir Francis Head, Governor-General of Canada, saying:

"In both the northern and southern hemispheres of the New World, Nature has not only outlined her works on a larger scale, but has painted the whole picture with brighter and more costly colors than she used in delineating and in beautifying the Old World. The heavens appear infinitely higher, the sky is bluer, the air is fresher, the cold is intenser, the moon looks larger, the stars are brighter, the wind is stronger, the rain is heavier, the rivers longer, the forests bigger, the plains broader."

But to forget about the ravage and enjoy what is left, get a walking stick. It is vital to walking. Thorsten Veblen once said it served the purpose of an advertisement that the bearer's hands are employed otherwise than in useful effort, and it has utility as an evidence of leisure.

JOGGING

Nowhere in the world is there such a continuous battle of the bulge as in well-fed America. Diets and exercises of extraordinary kinds come to prominence and are quickly adopted as fads. They usually last a few weeks or months and then fade away, leaving the authors fat with royalties.

The latest pursuit of pound-conscious men and women is jogging. The over-weight don track suits and shoes and proceed at a jogging pace around parks or deserted raceways. Those who are self-conscious about public exhibition are advised to stand in the same place at home and try jogging without going anywhere. The theory seems to be that if you jolt and jar the flab around enough it will shrink or be pounded away.

In a recent American election campaign, a Detroit congressman, John F. Boyle, became known as "Jack the Jogger." In doing so, he added a gimmick to the spectacle of American politics and avoided costly handouts, which almost immediately become part of the great American litter.

"Jack the Jogger" invited voters to jog around supermarket plazas with him. When they stopped the 34-year-old campaigner gave them a rousing speech while they were still too tired to move. He said it saved him money on advertising because the phenomenon was still so new that the newspapers are covering his jogs.

14 *November*

NOVEMBER

November is a time of treasures in drab settings. Berries are drops of fire and blood against greys and browns. Crows have doffed their dusty September coats for jet black costumes that will gleam like ebony in the coming white of winter.

The blue jays flicker amongst grey tree limbs in startling blue and white. Downy woodpeckers sport fall outfits with overtones of fashionable tweed. The cardinals are moving exclamation points of red.

High in the grey sky of evening comes a clamor of gabbling. A man on his way home stops to listen and watch. Then he will see a close V-formation of Canada geese. It is the true voice of autumn as the honkers move like a rippling series of perforations across the sky.

The watcher stands in the haunting memory of the sight as the sound fades. He knows as he moves towards the beacon of his home that they are following the sun. Until he reaches the warmth of his own destination, he is impaled on the sadness of the moment.

MEMORIES

City dwellers, transplanted by ambition and time from country hills and valleys, live with poignant memories in November. They remember stark, frost-held nights when hounds bayed at treed coons by the side of corn-stubbled fields.

They yearn for the mellow warmth of farm kitchens, fragrant from spicy pumpkin pie and fresh-made sausage flavored with newly dried sage. They ache for the tang of a fall apple, still chilled by autumnal frost.

Men, weary from traffic battles, stand still on their suburban plots and listen enviously to the freedom call of migrant birds, winging high overhead on their way south. Women switch off television sets, uneasily aware of the transparency of the adventure in the face of the reality of gathering Arctic disturbances and turbulence in the Dakotas and Montana.

Old men who appear to be dozing in comfort are living in memory. The November wind is a prompter that makes them relive youthful exploits, when cold and snow were adversaries in bitter but triumphant battles for survival.

NOVEMBER MOOD

November is unpredictable. It sun-sparkles and yet, feminine-like, can turn almost sombre to match the overtones of a brown landscape, where stems, twigs and stalks stand out like coppered filigree.

It is a time of soft tones where stubborn apples cling to bared branches, wizened and wrinkled and brown. Nestling windfalls take on the protective coloration of seared grass. Milkweed leaves are leather-tanned. Wild carrot, more dignified as Queen Anne's lace, has clenched its doily-like blooms into rust-shaded tangles.

With a Midas touch, squirrels are busy filling larders with

nuts, many of which they will absentmindedly leave, and so
help the plan of propagation. Boys probe amongst waves of
fallen leaves for chestnuts for most serious purposes, and
mothers, coming across the forgotten hoardings in dresser
drawers and jacket pockets, will also aid nature by returning
them to the bosom of earth.

Days which begin with sunlight may progress through hazi-
ness, veils of misty rain and even intermittent scatterings of
snow. Man is a mere bystander at the convulsive happenings
of the brown and moody month of November.

STORM WINDOWS

What strange propensity lurks in man to make him delay
installing his storm windows? He knows from experience that
they must be hung each Fall and yet finds excuse after excuse
for postponing the task.

Wives use guile by commenting on the prudence of a neighbor: "Bert certainly gets ready for the winter. He has his
garden all redded up and he even put the storm windows on.
Alice says she never had to mention it to him."

It doesn't work, so the housekeeper pointedly makes a pro-
duction of polishing the objects in question. She may even
make threatening gestures as if she might install them herself.
The average man is not to be taken in by such a ruse.

He remains immune to the suggestions of an early winter,
but as time passes he may make minor concessions. These
consist usually of an inspection of the screens which first have
to be removed. He finds little inspiration, but under pressure
will promise action on a subsequent Saturday.

He always has an excuse on the promised day. The boss has
arranged a golf game with a client. He has to take the car in
for winterizing. He usually ends up watching a football game
on TV, seemingly unperturbed by dark looks and muttered
threats.

Then on a day when the wind has ice on its teeth and is
smothered in sleety rain, he is forced to struggle with the win-

dows. His hands are numbed, the ladder is slippery and his temper is vile. A wise wife forbears reminding him of the pleasant days when the task would have been so easy.

Give the poor man the benefit of the doubt. He was probably glorying in autumnal weather and couldn't bear to shut it out, even with storm windows.

FLAME OF THE CITY

"The larger our great cities grow, the more irresistible becomes the attraction which they exert on the children of the country, who are fascinated by them as the birds are fascinated by the lighthouse or the moths by the candle." — Havelock Ellis.

Since 1945, North and South America have been privy to a mass exodus of country people to city living. Responding to pressures beyond their understanding they trek from farms and small towns to crowd into urban areas. Some make the transition happily, but a great many are forced to accept conditions infinitely worse than those they left.

In South America the favelas are stinking masses of humanity packed in under appalling conditions of poverty and sanitation. The Negroes of the South crowd the tenements and ghettos of the Northern United States. In Canada, thousands of families from subsistence farms and from towns where industry has evaporated attempt to compete in circumstances they didn't anticipate.

Why do they come?

The industrialization of farming is one reason. Men, ill equipped at any time to farm, managed to exist before efficiency was introduced to agriculture. Some moved because they were unable to educate their families properly and felt that the city would make it easier. Television gives many of them a false picture of city conditions. They become absorbed in the unreal world of people who never seem to work and yet enjoy the best of all possible worlds. The country moth is lured by the city flame!

Country people have little real knowledge of cities. One transplanted villager saw it as "just a place where people live closer together. There's not as much space." They are unaware of tensions, values, social groups and the fact that living in cities shapes the outlook of the people over a period of time.

The new resident may even have money by country standards but he finds it inadequate if he wants to live in the suburbs, his first choice. Step by step he looks at the sections where he would like to live, finding the same cold reality of soaring prices and high down payments. He settles inevitably in a run-down sector, where living accommodation is dominated by greed, and he is in effect competing with long-time occupants.

When a man goes to look for work carrying the qualifications of "steady worker with a good strong back and willing hands," he encounters all kinds of obstacles. He hasn't a trade or a skill. Even in the field of construction work he is competing with a vested interest group. He doesn't understand unions and he finds them often as difficult to comprehend as industries which scorn "hard work" for training. For the first time in his life he is dealing with strangers, and all of them want money from him in schemes and devices for getting him employed. Duped once or twice, he becomes wary and distrustful even of patient employment officials.

The city, with its noise and crowded downtown conditions, becomes a jungle in place of a haven. His wife, alarmed in the first place by having been cajoled into buying furniture and household necessities on "easy term" credit, begins to hate her surroundings. She still wears respectability as a shield and finds many of the other women in the apartment block or tenement to be callous and worldly. The children, marked as outsiders at school and play, must either demonstrate their acceptance of slum values and codes or be forever persecuted.

The husband starts the weary round of occasional work. He

is exploited by labor contractors on non-union jobs. There comes the inevitable time when his wife finds it easier to get work than he does. It's low paying and often menial, but steady. His sense of manliness and his pride in "being a good worker" begins to give way, and he can't face the days of being cooped in small rooms doing household work.

Soon the television set becomes an "electronic baby-sitter." He spends more time away from home, in daydreaming, fitting in with a group who find communal solace in deploring misfortune. He constructs his elaborate plans for a small business or for taking a trade course to take home at night as a peace offering to his tired wife. Soon the family doesn't pay any attention to him, and he knows he is not really important any more.

The country ties of a church and knowledge that the community would help in an emergency are gone. Nightly in the neighborhood there are fights, infidelities and children involved in petty crime. For the first time in his life the man must keep quiet about everything, maintain a stolid silence with all authority and relinquish all his inherited country values.

In the crowded, hot room there is no privacy. The streets are merely places of overflow from the crowded dwelling places. He longs for the open country and freedom, and when he starts frequenting a park he becomes an object of attention for the police. In time he becomes a gray shadow, trying to avoid the attention of his wife, his family, which is beginning to break up and drift away, creditors, landlords and officials of all kinds.

Somehow any study of cities undertaken by federal authorities must include reasonable consideration of how to flameproof the wings of the country innocents who each year test the candle flame of the city.

TIME OF THE OWLS

As we edge toward winter and nights crisp with cold, the mysterious owls make their presence known to man. They were here all the time but as the other night noises subside their lonely calls are given emphasis.

Listen carefully in the country or even in some of the sub-urban areas and you will be able to identify the species. Each owl has a characteristic in the forlorn accent of the hooting. The barred and great horned ones sound deep and gruff. The screech owl starts on a high, wailing note and wavers down.

A countryman pushing through the night veil of cold, when even the moon appears as a frozen sphere, may shiver at the sound of an owl hooting. A shadowy glimpse of the solemn fellow with hooked beak and fierce eyes does little to melt the stab of fear.

Yet there need be no fear. The owls are friends of man, waging relentless war on pestering rodents. The hooting is not a warning to humans. It may announce resident and terri-torial rights to other residents. Again, it may be a romantic prelude to mid-winter courtship and domesticity. It is a true and natural sound of the cold time abdicated by less hardy breeds of birds — the time of the owls.

15 *December*

DECEMBER

December is a month of expectation. Youngsters test new slopes for skiing and tobogganing and hope that ponds and rivers will ice quickly for skating. Grey days are followed by sunny ones. Snow comes and vanishes uneasily. Winter has not yet become a permanent feature.

December is a month of limited daylight. Yet, the fifteen hours of darkness is in many ways a pleasant happening. Night seems to glow in this month, and the trees and shrubs stand out in sharply-etched silhouettes. Houselights are gentle beacons of warmth. A distant town or city illuminates the sky in a way that rivals the glory of Northern Lights.

December mornings contain surprises for the awakened sleeper. Soft spells follow frigid ones. Rain develops out of snowfalls. Bare ground may be covered overnight by a counterpane of snow. There is no rigid grip of prolonged days of cold or blizzards in this month of change.

December is tempered by the knowledge of Christmas to come.

COUNTRY STILLNESS

City dwellers should be compensated at some point each winter for endurance of daily noise and din with a sampling of winter stillness in the country. This is not silence! It's a soothing sense of quiet punctuated only by natural sounds.

In the woods the jays are subdued, and stubborn leaves still clinging to trees rustle in a gentle, conspiratorial way. Creeks and ponds are congealed by ice. Where running water has escaped the embrace of frost it gurgles. In deep swamps the crows have forsaken their warm weather boisterousness. Under the eaves the sparrows chitter, and high in the barn mows the pigeons burble in a low-pitched way.

By nightfall, cabins by iced lakes or farm houses nestling beside protective hedges twinkle with light against the contrast of snow and dark sky. Stand and listen. Simple sounds have identity, from the far off bark of a dog to the nearby swish of a pine tree.

It is the time of stillness, when you can hear the quiet and recuperate from the assaults of violent, ugly, urban noise. Enjoy the relief while you can. There is evidence that man has designs on his drawing board to rupture it. When sonic booms blast our country stillness, can outdoor Muzak by satellite be far behind?

WINTER WIND

The wind of December is a busybody with a cold breath. It seems to concern itself constantly with pushing us into deep winter. It is a noisy ogre without redeeming features such as those enjoyed by the breezes of other seasons.

This wind scurries up and down the hillsides, rattling the scarce leaves on dejected-looking trees. It pokes in crevices and cracks and whistles eerily around eaves. The storm windows rattle and loosely hatched doors flap as a part of the chilly song.

A December wind glories in snow. The landscape is still bare enough that the snow can be piled and repiled, shifted and shunted, and above all pelted at the weary traveller. Listen carefully during one of those freak storms and you'll hear the fantastic song of the December wind.

January will bring the deep cold when even the wind must be still, so we just allow the December wind time now to romp and play. Perhaps it is not an ogre, but really an agent of nature trying to temper us for the frigid tests which are yet to come.

THE CHRISTMAS TREE

Fortunate the child who has the opportunity to accompany a thoughtful parent on an expedition to select a Christmas tree. Luckier still, the child privileged to make a trip to the country, beyond the bundled trees on the sales lots and the ersatz ones gleaming with plastic heartiness in stores.

A romp through a snowy field up a hillside punctuated by conical fir, balsam or cedar trees is the beginning of a memory fit for a lifetime. To be allowed the pleasure of choice and then to assist in the sawing or cutting of the focal article for the Christmas celebration is in itself assurance of the success of the holiday.

A tree brought sparkling from natural surroundings gives an aura and aroma of the season. Decorated and illuminated it somehow retains the atmosphere of crisp air and star-studded skies. A child in the presence of such a tree can easily imagine, even in a contradictory world, the solemn mystery of shepherds on a hillside, a guiding star for the distant magi and the heaven-resounding message of "Peace on earth, good will toward men."

WOMEN SHOPPERS

Let any man foolish enough to treasure the myth of women as members of a weaker sex, enter the lists for the Christmas jousting in any large department store. If he emerges capable of speech he will be filled with awe and wonderment.

There is some quality which endows a woman in the pre-Christmas days and makes her almost super-human. Women, ordinary, sweet, pleasant-seeming women, flow from buses, cars and subways clutching containers for loot, half crouching as they move in guerrilla stance. Once inside, they stalk down the passageways between the counters with the intensity of plague locusts in harvest fields.

A man cannot compete against their handling of weaponry such as umbrellas, shopping bags, enormous, lethal purses and of course . . . elbows! Women's elbows must be the most terrifying armament in the world next to the sharpened, bamboo stakes of the Viet Cong.

They ignore the rules. A man may be uncomfortable waiting for the eye of the sales clerk, but he obeys the custom of taking turns. Then, just as he almost gets attention, a woman shopper will supercede him, without apology or apparent acknowledgement of his existence.

Ottawa sources say former Prime Minister Pearson did his Christmas shopping from samples at his office. This may account for a certain naïvete in setting up a Royal Commission concerning the equality of women. It's obvious he hasn't had to compete with them at Christmas shopping.

SNOW

Somehow snow is the symbol which remains identified with Canada. We complain about it, scorn it as a chilly plague and plan winter abdications to warmer climates.

Each fall we glory in the color, and we treasure Indian summer while anticipating the white stuff with a certain dread. Conversation is dominated by dreaming of retirement to sun-drenched islands, where snow seems like a myth of imagination.

Then it comes whirling out of a grey sky, covering the tired landscape of the country. It spills on the city gardens and parks and puffs up like icing on the nooks and crannies of yesterday's architecture, but slithers helplessly down the flat and gilded sides of today's buildings.

For a time, before traffic and fumes reduce it to a dark, murky mass, we glory in it. It causes us to dream dreams of childhood, of snowball fights and frolic. Momentarily, imagination can make us hear the sound of happy yelling and the melodious jingle-jangle of sleigh and cutter bells above the raucous discord of noise so typical of the modern city.

This first snow is usually only a warning, but it brings a happy hope of rewards on distant hills and ice-stilled ponds and streams. For most of us, the lure of sun-drenched islands and tropical retirement will never materialize. Yet, there is reason to believe that if it did, our affair with a twelve-month summer could not remain constant. Snow, the winter habit, has marked us deeply.

COLD WEATHER

Cold weather is inevitable in December. Nature feints with thrusts of cold, irregular snowfalls, softening winds and stretches of sunshine, as part of the pre-winter game. Then, as we relax with old myths about open winters caused by dwindling ice caps, an assault force of cold strikes.

It may come at the time of the Beaver moon, the full one of December, in the days when fields are polluted by droves of trigger-happy city hunters, or in the somewhat euphoric pre-Christmas time.

The furnace roars into an all night defensive action, signifying that the iron fist is tightening outside. In undefended homes without central heating you can tell by the splintering and groaning sounds of frost-held wood how intense the attack really is. That's when men with numbed fingers try to coax reluctant stoves into battle operations.

Outside the air is almost stiff with the cold. A deep inhalation produces a knife-like reaction in tender lungs, and the vapor of breath rides in the crisp atmosphere like cartoon balloons waiting for blasphemous and angry words. Icy fingers pry into clothing apertures and stab at warm skin.

The countryman gears his pace to survival and moves briskly. His ambition is to return to a warm household as quickly as possible. Once within the comforting embrace of heat, there is time to reflect that it is only a foretaste of the extremes a Canadian winter is certain to provide during January and February.

THE GIVING GAME

It's a game played by wives and husbands in the weeks leading up to Christmas.

"Please tell me what you want for Christmas."

Husbands are generally evasive.

"Oh, I don't really want anything. This Christmas present thing is a lot of nonsense."

The wife doesn't believe him.

"Come on now, tell me or at least give me a hint of what you want."

"Look, if there's anything I need I can get it for myself."

That's the rub for most people in today's affluent society. An increasing number of people are swimming in consumer goods, but they're caught in the ritual of Christmas. It's part of the seasonal pattern, bearing little or no relationship to religious or Christian inheritance. Christmas is for giving! That's the message dinned at us from all corners beginning, it seems, earlier each Fall season.

"There must be something you really want, George."

Of course there's something the husband wants, but chances are he will not tell. Instead of confessing secret dreams for a new over-and-under, 12-gauge shotgun or a snazzy sheepskin jacket with genuine buffalo horn buttons and leather thongs, he'll keep on being evasive.

On Christmas morning, while the family maunders through bundles and parcels and oceans of wrapping, he'll gallantly join them by opening his assortment of shirts, ties, socks, cigars, gloves, scarves, underwear and the occasional whimsicality such as an orange and blue moustache cup. Muttering polite thanks and reflecting on the vast and exciting presents his family are enjoying and what it's costing, he may think longingly of the shotgun and the woolly sheepskin jacket.

His wife would have dampened his enthusiasm by saying he was only dreaming because he wasn't a sportsman. At least he wasn't what she thought a sportsman might be, as illustrated in those wonderful magazine ads with the lean, tanned, handsome men gazing skywards with steely, blue eyes.

If he could have only been truthful:

"Look, I want a shotgun and a jacket like that because when I was a boy growing up in Moose Pasture, Manitoba, I used to dodge along when the others went hunting and I didn't have a gun and I was half-frozen in an old windbreaker of my dad's that was four sizes too big. So maybe I would only use them a few times but, man, it would be so nice to own them."

Take my word for it, tell the truth, men! Your family may think you're a bit daft, but it will be a genuine relief to have you at least give them a clue as to what you want, down in your heart of hearts. Last summer, for instance, while teaching in Banff at the Fine Arts School I fell in love with a set of brass, counter-scale weights in the window of an antique store. They were graduated and slightly ugly and only $28.00.

I started walking by the shop every morning. The attendant began to watch me as a suspicious character. When they vanished from the window, I rushed in, filled with apprehension.

"Are you a weight collector?" smiled the clerk, showing the weights which had been moved to an inside shelf.

I fingered the weights and murmured something about just liking their shape. They became a kind of obsession and I kept on talking about them. I left Banff without buying, but still lamenting why I didn't.

Why didn't I? For the same reason I suspect that most men will not tell the truth about what they want for Christmas.

Part of the drift to urban life from farms and small towns, we Depression veterans still have hangovers of memory where it concerns buying for ourselves.

Nostalgia moved me to the weights. They reminded me of my father's general store and of the brass-panned balance scales used to weigh spices and smaller articles. Nostalgia also pointed out that they were unnecessary and would only be dust collectors in my office.

On the other hand, if someone I knew had expressed a desire for them, the $28 and the memory would not stop me for a moment from buying. I'm not alone. This philosophy tinges all kinds of decisions.

"Men are cheapskates about themselves," says Sidney Goodwill, who manages men's departments for his store in Ottawa and Montreal. "They'll buy their wives and girl friends everything. They buy their wives a $250 party dress to wear a few times and they won't buy themselves a good $150 suit they wear 150 times. The bills come first."

So, what about Christmas gifts for men? After diligent cross-examination of a tremendous variety of middle-aged, fairly prosperous men, some facts emerge. Most men don't want gifts of clothing. In spite of the fact that women buy 70 percent of men's clothing for them in North America, they still don't welcome clothing on Christmas morning. Girl friends are better at picking out clothing than wives. A girl friend will imagine the man to be dark, handsome and more romantic looking than he is and purchase exotica such as Russian-style pajamas, turtle neck sweaters, bright ascots and racing driver gloves. Wives see their husbands as bigger than they actually are, and end up with clothes several sizes too large.

Dr. Ernest Dichter of the Institute of Motivational Research plumps for cigars:

"There is a sense of self indulgence when you light up a cigar. It is a conscious demonstration of enjoyment. A man smoking a cigar is expressing a feeling that his enjoyment is complete, without anyone else, just he and his cigar. This attention and companionship may be a source of women's rejection of cigars generally, for it arouses a form of jealousy."

If you must buy clothes for your husband, then try woollens. The motivational research people found that it has a connotation of the outdoors for men. It conjures for them visions of piney woods, lodges, red woollen shirts, tobacco smoke, tweeds, ivy covered colleges. It is masculine, in a man's view, sexually attractive, sedate, conservative and cultured. It makes men feel capable of coping with the outdoors, and it is a symbol of respectable group life.

A Calgary oil engineer refused to admit he was reluctant to tell his family what he wanted as a gift. He called a week later to say, "There is something I've wanted. I would like a soft, woolly rug for beside the bed. I want to feel it on my feet the last thing when I go to bed and the first thing when I get up in the morning."

Why didn't he say that?

"It would sound silly. I spend six months of every year living in bunkhouses and tents. Besides, I'm sure my wife would say it clashed with the decor of the bedroom."

Why did he really want it?

"I've searched my mind ever since we talked and all I can think of is that my grandfather had one in the spare bedroom where I used to go on visits and, man, did it ever feel good."

And what about a pool table? Great! Every man has a secret vision of himself as someone with the skill of a Minnesota Fats but without the girth.

Now, there is another reason for a man liking a pool table. The poolroom used to be a deliciously safe but somewhat dubious spot as a hangout when he was in high school or college. Women frowned on it as a black spot of profanity, smoking and girlie pictures. It was, and it was a refuge, but it was an all-male proposition. Most men now feel a trifle uneasy about democratising pool into a family sport, so if you have visions of buying your husband a pool table and equipment and then setting it up in a room with frilly curtains where you can take company for a social evening, you'd better forget it. Well, at least leave the room a trifle dark, so that the green shaded lamp casts a pool of light on the table, let him do the inviting and above all let it have a masculine touch. A cigar store Indian might do the trick, if you can find one!

Men enjoy wooden objects. They like the solid looking fact of wood and take pleasure in handling them.

"I take a real kick out of tools and especially power tools," said a Montreal teacher. "The trouble is, your family expects you to use them. It gets a bit silly cutting a $2 board with a $100 power saw. The other point is women are becoming the handymen. They watch do-it-yourself shows, buy books on repairing and, if you procrastinate, you'll come home to find your wife with all the power tools spread out building a new recreation room."

Don't be too sure your husband really wants a bigger and better barbecue! There's evidence he would like to be rid of the whole thing.

"We live in the suburbs," says one victim, "and the Saturday night barbecue has become a farce. While the guests are enjoying themselves the poor bloody husband who was once fascinated by the idea of cooking outdoors tries to frizzle up more elaborate recipes on equipment that's getting as complicated as the ranges of the Queen Elizabeth hotel. I'd settle for crystal, table cloth and a good roast in a pleasant dining room anytime."

The penurious background of men makes them hesitant when spending money on themselves. A new car, a houseboat, a trailer or a sailboat can be excused on the grounds that the purchase is for the enjoyment of the entire family.

Men have quirks. One man complained that he had never had a son to buy an electric train for, and he hesitated to buy one for his daughter. He admitted he wanted it for himself. What if his wife presented him with a model train?

"I'd be flabbergasted but I'd be pleased."

Retailers say that more and more women are turning to

men's toiletries as gifts. It is one of the most rapidly expanding items of retail sales in North America. Men are divided about them. They admit that toiletries are suitable and yet they have some reluctance, as they think of them as "sissy."

Part of the problem of what to give father may be caused by the change in status. In the good old days, father accepted his shirt and socks and five cigars and sat around content in the knowledge that through his hard work his family was enjoying a happy if modest Christmas.

It's different today. Mother is probably a working woman as well. Bernard DeVoto, noting the fact, said, "What every career woman needs is a good wife." A poll shows that more than one-third of husbands in the industrialized sections of North America do the dishes, clean the house and look after children. The Gallup poll insists that 62 percent of American husbands are on intimate terms with dishwater, and 40 percent help with the cooking . . . and not just barbecuing for visitors.

But women will still probably keep on buying clothes for men and men will stoically accept. They'll admit to another man they would like at least one Saville Row suit, following Clifton Webb who said, "English tailors make clothes for gentlemen."

The matter of clothes is really discouraging.

"The average man," says Russell Lynes, "is an eccentric along with millions of eccentrics, but unlike the true eccentric he has a problem of protective coloring. He wants to be different, but not really different. He wants to express personality as he sees it, but he does not want to give himself away. He wants to be in fashion but he shudders at the idea of being fashionable. The truth is that he wants to be neither mass produced nor lonely, so he seeks solace in being some of both."

But women have their problems as well. The wife of a journalist relates her troubles in buying her husband a smoking jacket, having him wear it once and then go back to an old sweater. He needed a hat so she bought the best she could and he wore it to a funeral and went back to a slouch job that must have been inherited from Noah.

"Then one day in front of a hi-fi shop he sighed and said he would like a good playback. The following Monday I went to that place and made the mistake of asking for a phonograph. They looked at me as if I was a profaner of a sacred temple and said they only sold sound systems. I persisted and was drowned in sound and words about tweeters, woofers, resistance, output and all kinds of gobbledygook about fidelity, which I thought had something to do with marriage. All I could do was ask Bill to go and pick out what he wanted. He just looked at me and said there were a lot of other things we needed that were more important for the house, and that's when I gave up. He's getting shirts and socks and underwear because I know he needs them, and he'll sit there on Christmas morning looking like an old sheep dog deserted by his master. I'll feel bad but there's nothing I can do about it."

Oh yes, the brass weights!

Recently I found them hidden in the back of a clothes closet among a cache of Christmas presents. So you see, men, there's nothing like being open and truthful when you hear that question, "What do you want for Christmas?"

CHRISTMAS EVE

In spite of invasions of the privacy of the moon, stereophonic blasting of Christmas carols and suggested rabbit-fur tablecloths as presents, this season still has a reward. It is never more apparent than in the late, quiet houses of Christmas Eve.

When the last parcel has been wrapped and placed beneath the tree, mother has time to rest. The visitors have gone. The children have subsided restlessly into sleep. Father has given up puttering and supervising and gone off to bed.

The lady of the house, like a good general on the eve of

battle, reviews her tactical plans for the coming struggle. Having satisfied herself of preparations she has an interlude for thoughts and memories.

Christmas past floods in. She remembers the expectancy of Christmas in her childhood, the association of evergreens and holly, of crisp nights when stars blazed, and the tantalizing scents of spice and food.

In these moments of quiet and remembrance, there must come the realization of the mystery of Christmas. It is a continuing fact that the spirit of the festival lies in giving rather than receiving. The shepherds of the nearby hills gave homage and the kings from distant lands brought costly gifts as well.

A mother in the still of Christmas Eve knows the full measure of the lesson of giving, and in her own way is rewarded.

16   *The Changeless Magic*

Thirty-odd years ago my generation abdicated the farms and friendly hamlets of Canada for the cities. Droves of us made up a migration. Our suits were too big, our caps were conspicuous, and we carried black, painted, cardboard suitcases. We went to school and war and work. Most of us stayed, because the city was a kind of dream. Today the dream is hazy. The years have caught up, and while the reality of the city is hazy with pollution and annoying with noise, we've started dreaming about where we started. It's easy to remember the musty, salt smell of the Tantramar Marsh, the gentle beauty of prairie roses and the sounds of migrating birds in flyway refuges. A lone tree bedecked in color can make us ache for the Laurentian and Haliburton highlands. Wood smoke can send a heart reeling for the Cariboo Country or Jasper, or a note in the whistling wind can bring an ache for salt-faded cottages in Ferrydale or Seldom Come By. But the worst time of all is Christmas Eve!

Every transplanted country person has a Christmas Eve memory of a small place. There was a magical transformation at that time. A pimple of houses and stores on the railroad line could become a bedazzling metropolis. It was a fairyland of lights, sleighs, bells, stores, presents, people, and above all, the joy of wonderful anticipation.

Are they still out there? As the noise increases and the snow churns to black pulp on the crowded city streets, we wonder about the little places and what is happening on Christmas Eve. Can there be anything but open space and a few super-farms remaining out beyond that tidal wave of conforming houses and black tarmacked shopping centres? Do they still have roads? They must, although the lava ribbons of super-highways ignore them. Not altogether, but there's a conde-scending note about LOWETOWN — 3 MLS — GAS — FOOD — LODGING. The superhighwaymen, who push their roads across swamps, fields and through forests so as to avoid any sign of habitation, grudgingly admit the presence of the small places. If you're forced to, you can get gas, food and accommodation down that narrow, misty road, but hurry back. This road goes to big and important places. Small places are for sleeping!

But small places do exist, and they do have some of that magic on Christmas Eve. You have to get away from the con-taminating influence of suburbs and big cities and frontier-style, one-storey stores in shopping plazas. You have to find a Main Street with a few gaps in it, like the irregular grin of a child with second teeth coming in. They've had a few casu-alties, and one or two places were not replaced after the fire 40 years ago, before they bought the new pumper and engine for the volunteer fire department.

Don't expect it to be exactly the same. There are changes but the Christmas lights look the same. They're strung from pole to pole to pole and droop across the centre and have pendants that are very much like the ones . . . that . . . oh, but they couldn't be.

"Remember those lights?"

"Yes, but surely . . ."

"We had to replace quite a few but they're the same. Tom Wilson, in the hardware, was on the council and he found out the factory was going out of business so he bought up their whole stock. We got enough to last . . . well . . . I guess as long as this burgh will last." That's the chief of police. He was one of the ones who stayed. "What are you doing Christmas Eve?"

His car has a siren and a two-way radio. There's no central dispatcher because there's only one other man on the force but Lil Hardy at Telephone Central can cut in on him and give him any messages.

"George McKenzie. You know Red Dan McKenzie's boy. He went to the Mounties for a time but came home. He's ordinarily the night man but his kids are small and I figure he should be home with them on a night like this. Besides, I like working on Christmas Eve. My son works in Ottawa and the girl will be home in the morning. She's in Montreal. Kind of wish Joe would come home and bring the grandchildren. Miss not having any kids around on Christmas Day."

The car is warm and parked beside the town hall. The snow falls like goose feathers, drifting down lazily. The perfect way for a Christmas Eve. Chief Albert Prideau puts on the wipers and cuts a semi-circle of wet cleanness.

"Listen."

He cuts in on the police band and listens for a few minutes. They're busy. Cars and accidents and traffic jam-ups down on that snooty superhighway. He's proud of the radio.

"Big help to us, you know."

He doesn't explain. He obviously likes some kinds of progress. His office is still in the basement of the town hall in front of the two cells. He has a wash basin of his own, but has to use the public Gents. The town council has been promising him a bathroom for years. It gets in the estimates, but when time comes to pare down the taxes it always seems to get taken out, with a promise he'll get it for sure the following year.

As the car noses out down the main street there are changes. Several snowmobile contraptions, sassy-looking and bright colored, and only an occasional sleigh. People stream back and forth across the street, laughing and talking a lot. Out at the end of the main street, as if it had been placed there by municipal purpose, the one supermarket is full of people. Against the sky, barely within sighting distance, is the big bulk of the drive-in screen now closed and winter-vacant.

There are plenty of customers at the supermarket but a lot still go to the gaunt, red brick building which says MACDON-ALD'S DEPT. STORE EST'B 1889. They come because of habit and credit, and perhaps because there has been a Mac-donald on the village council since 1901. It's sad in a way to think that when Bert leaves the council he'll be the last one. Both his sons are lawyers in Toronto. For a time people hoped Tom might come back and practise, but he married a city girl, and as the chief notes, "It probably wouldn't work out. I think you have to be country bred to stay here."

He excuses himself and leaves you in charge of law and order and the car and radio as he goes into "Madeline's Ladies Wear Shoppe" and comes out carrying a parcel. Several other red-necked countrymen come out at the same time with parcels. It's easy to guess their wives will be getting presents bought with the advice of Madeline Simpson. There's an understanding on Christmas Eve that men stay away from the men's wear department of Macdonald's so that women can do their gift shopping. The women avoid going to Madeline's Shoppe.

"Guess I'll stay away from the poolroom. Lots of kids down from school and I don't want to spoil their fun. I can't see any harm in kids playing pool anyhow, but there's an old ordinance here . . ."

The recorded carols sound amazingly good from the radio

and repair shop. It used to be a harness shop, and people actually bought red pom-poms for their horse bridles to wear on Christmas Day.

Zinneman's Bakery is crowded, and the windows are all steamed up.

"Should take your family home some of Fred's good bread. It's still a lot better than that wrapped stuff."

The Lyceum movie theatre is forlorn. It's been boarded up since it yielded to the drive-in and television.

"I miss the theatre," muses the policeman, "always could slip in and see the new shows. Some good ones, too. Drive-in doesn't seem the same. I liked the smell of that theatre."

The door is open and he's out of the car. The children with snowballs are chased from in front of the War Memorial.

"That's one thing I won't stand for. I know it's been a long time, but I think the kids should be taught respect for a thing like that. I always make them skedaddle."

The hockey rink is blaring with noise and blue with smoke. Who can enforce a NO SMOKING sign in a place like that? They're frying onions in the little refreshment stand.

"Would you look at the length of those skirts?"

He chuckles all the way out.

"You know they tried to start a ruckus about these teeny skirts. Only a few old cranks, but I told the council I'd be damned if I would go around with a tape measure estimating those things. I'd get charged as a dirty old man or something."

We look in at Lee's Cafe. The juke box vibrates with that wailing, thumping cacophony of modern music, and denim-clad youngsters with pipestem legs are waving and twisting with girls wearing what seem to be even shorter skirts than the ones at the rink.

"Gotta use your head in a case like that. Charlie Lee's not complaining so why bother them. I don't get those dances. They just stand and shake at each other like snake charmers."

Lots of service stations. Six on Main Street and two on the way to the grist mill. They all seem to be busy. There's almost

as many service stations now as churches. Somebody calls out
"Chiefy" and he waves. There are other voices here as well.
These are foreign voices of red cheeked men and women with
little processions of children who move a little diffidently, as if
they had an edge of fear. He waves to them, and when he
speaks they all speak back. Something snaps in the moment
that had stretched tight with a minor tension.

"They're all back on the Ninth Concession or the River
road. Came in and took up the land of the people who sold
out when their families went away to work in the city. Good
people. Very respectful and, I think, a little afraid of a
uniform. I try to be a little extra pleasant with them. They're
good people!"

Old men sit in the lobby of the Queen's hotel. An unwatched
television set with a ghostly, dancing and untuned image flares
over the rumble of voices in the beverage room.

"Have a beer, Chief."

He shakes his head, but somehow he has memories as well.
For a few moments he stands in the hallway and smells the
yeasty aroma and stares up the dark stairs. It's empty up there
now because the burly hydro and highway crews have gone
home. The rooms are left with only memories of the drummers
with the fur-collared coats, who smelled of toilet water and
came around to spend days with the local merchants. The
rooms where they used to open their display trunks are now
occupied by a barber shop and a cobbler. The Queen's is really
only a shell around the beer parlor. Even the high-ceilinged
dining room with the great potted plants has been closed in
favor of a snack bar.

He's quite a civic booster.

"We got a florist now. Used to just have a Dutchman along
the river with a green house but this fellow has a place over
there where the smithy used to be. Quiet in the summer, so he
sells antiques to the few tourists who wander in here. Busy now
though."

After a time he adds wistfully, "You know why he's so busy? He's making up flowers for sons and daughters who want them sent as apologies for not coming home. We got one from Ottawa. Nice flowers but the wife cried a bit. I told her it was only natural for them to spend Christmas with his wife's folks."

It's only a moment. He grins at the cracks of light showing through the shuttered windows of the Cribbage Club quarters of the Volunteer Firemen.

"I expect every regulation of the liquor commission is being broken in there at this moment, but what the hell? It's Christmas Eve and they're good fellows. Saved the Presbyterian Church last year. Worked like Trojans. Of course, the new engine is a really fine one. I'd show it to you only I don't want to disturb them."

Lil Hardy cuts in on the radio, and he swings around and goes back to the hockey rink. It settles down, but he takes one boy to a corner and talks to him for a time and the boy shrugs his shoulders and leaves. The stores are closing up and he tries a few doors. The organ is playing at the Catholic Church before midnight mass and people are moving towards it. A lot of headlights are coming up from the side streets.

Lee's coffee tastes good and he takes a container in for Lil Hardy. He goes in the Public Gents, tries the door of the town hall and brings out a hamper from his office.

"We got a few people who find it slim pickings around this time of year so the Businessmen's Club gives out baskets."

He didn't elaborate. The railroad station is a dark, deserted island with no rails running to it.

"Gotta pick up a passenger."

A white powdered lump at the door is roused. A man comes mumbling, but without complaint, and gets in the back seat.

"I don't know what happened. I just felt tired, Bert, and sat down and I must have dozed off."

The Chief assures him everything is "okay" and rolls down

the window a bit. The beery smell is a little cloying. The porch light flicks on as he is helping the stumbling figure up the pathway to the little house. A whitehaired woman is framed in the open, lighted doorway.

"Amy, just gave Pete a lift here."

I can barely catch the words.

"At the station?"

"Yes, but it's Christmas Eve, Amy. Here's something we had left over and it'll only go to waste. I'd be obliged if you could use it." She thanks him with dignity and waits until he is in the car before closing the door.

"Pete's not a bad stick. Very little pension. Railroad had trouble with him. Gets a few pints in him now and he always ends up there, waiting for those trains that are never going to come again. Nice woman, Amy!"

The car noses along the straggling back streets where tall, mysterious houses stand beside ones with fishbowl windows disclosing people moving in party formations. It moves past the deserted refreshment drive-in stand and zips up the road to the superhighway. He parks at the cutoff and switches on the provincial call band.

The ribbons of light are never-ending as they stream in both directions. It seems as if there is even an earth vibration above that of the motor in the car. Horns are blowing, and trucks spread swathes of snow and slush. It has never seemed so frantically anxious, the whole thing punctuated by the calling back and forth about life and death and accident on the police radio. There's an interrupting signal and he switches.

"It's five to twelve, Albert, Merry Christmas."

He answers, "Thanks, Lil, and Merry Christmas to you."

He is turning the car around when he stops for a minute. Across the night comes the insistent banshee wail of sirens. He closes it off by running up the window.

"Boy, am I glad I'm here and not out there. Come on home with me. Have to wish the wife Merry Christmas. I'm on duty so you'll have to be the one to join her in Christmas eggnog."

A few stragglers were going to midnight mass, but the street was almost deserted. The big, glittering lighted sign with MERRY CHRISTMAS with the twisted letter T in it was still blazing. That was one thing that hadn't changed in spite of Tom Wilson buying out the whole stock of the factory. They mustn't have made any new T's because that's the way it was 30-odd years ago. Suddenly, I felt better. Little places still have a magic about them, especially on Christmas Eve.

17   *Peace for the Family of Man*

Memory makes past Christmas seasons appear as occasions of joyous simplicity. Families trooped home to evergreen-decorated houses fragrant with the spice of cooking. Children were obedient creatures eagerly accepting oranges, nuts and hand-carved toys along with their implicit belief in Santa Claus. The wassail bowl flowed in an astonishing way, while candlelight gleamed on happy faces and wreaths of holly.

The passing years mix truth and fiction. Wassail bowls existed mostly in Dickens or carols. Mother was an over-worked slave for hordes of family and relatives and their friends. Houses were drafty and a lot of them burned down when candles fell into the picturesque evergreen decorations. Children lacked perfection even in those halcyon days.

There is nothing wrong with pleasant and comforting memories. The problem exists when they are used for "dropping out" of the present. For instance, how many times will the analogy of Christ being born in the reign of Augustus, and of "The Old Romans" collapsing only five centuries later, be used in the current season as a dire omen of our situation?

Christmas has changed because man has changed. Our physical world may be frightening, but it is for a growing number of people infinitely more satisfying and comfortable than ever before. Plastic and baubles may not please a memory-nourished generation, but spruce trees are still available and it takes only effort to make popcorn balls.

Man has progressed in matters of the spirit as well. He is becoming aware that retreat into religious mysticism does not relieve his responsibility to fellow human beings. A donation to a charitable fund or a seasonal hamper does not excuse concern for the balance of the year. Divisive walls, often only barriers of bigotry for organized religion, are crumbling under ecumenical pressure.

There is an emerging realism in the search by young people for identity and purpose. If they bear no loyalty to legend they are also prepared not to compromise the present or the future.

We are all pinioned on the hinge of change. At times it is uncomfortable and pinching, but it is at least not paralyzing. Comfortable assumptions are constantly attacked by new volatilities.

Yet, in this time of change, an amazing power remains in the Christmas story of Bethlehem. It links the continuing hope of man for an eternal life in a commonality embracing kings and shepherds. The scene in the stable reminds us that there is a family of man, joined by the mystery of creation as symbolized in the birth of the Infant Jesus.

Christmas must represent hope for the future in place of retreat into the past. The collapse of an ancient civilization must not be accepted as an inevitable forecast of our fate.

Classics scholar Edith Hamilton wrote:

> "Our mechanical and industrial age is the only material achievement that can be compared with

Rome's during the two thousand years in between. It is worth our while to perceive that the final reason for Rome's defeat was the failure of mind and spirit to rise to a new and great opportunity, to meet the challenge of new and great events."

The new and great events are upon us, but a constant challenge remains in one vital rule ignored by the Romans. It was enunciated by former Prime Minister L. B. Pearson in his Reith lectures for the BBC as a dedication to the pursuit of Peace For The Family Of Man. This is in reality only a restatement of the moral and lesson of the Christmas story of Bethlehem.

Postscript

"One small step . . .
one giant step . . ."

Two men walked on the face of the moon while a third orbited in a space taxi to give them transport back to earth. Because we live in an age of technology, the event, transmitted live by television, was somewhat robbed of the heartbursting sense of adventure which lesser exploits caused when life was much simpler.

The progression of Man from the comfort of mythology to the practical realities of scientific development increases his respect for individuals. The heartening point for humanity was the concern of millions for the astronauts. It managed to persist in the face of what appeared to be a determination on the part of television to make it a scientific carnival. How many people would have appreciated the reasoned concerns of Reverend Ralph Abernathy in place of the impromptu interviews at Disneyland?

There were overtones of caution in the statements of the scientists who commented. Normally, science is accused of wanting to push ahead at all costs. Apollo 11, however, made many scientists suggest the folly of the rivalry between America and Russia. Bertrand Russell was chilling in his warning about transporting earth follies to the moon.

America today has an accomplishment of historic and shattering consequence. It came from a political decision made by a now-martyred American president. Surely it is not negative fact, but one to be remembered, that the capability to deliver the astronauts came from the development of the V-2 rockets of Peenemunde and the post war determination of Stalin to be able to bomb America.

While historical factors should not rob the present event of our fullest praise, they cannot be entirely forgotten. There was little reassurance in the gesture by Congress to allow only the American flag on the moon, excluding the world symbolism of the United Nations.

The deepest hope for a world starved for some form of symbolism, or of harmony in place of selfishness and narrow nationalism, came from the astronauts. They were humble, if joyous. Captain Armstrong said:

> "One small step for a man,
> One giant leap for mankind."

With those two lines, he demonstrated a close understanding of his fellow human beings. It seemed also as if he, unlike Congress, understood that the great leap had reduced earth to being only a constituency in the world of space.

PaperJacks

WITH A PINCH OF SIN
by Harry J. Boyle

It's the turn of the century and a young boy is growing up in the small rural town of Clover. It's a vibrant life, only one or two generations removed from the Frontier, where the Methodists and the Catholics eternally feud and the church-going people work hard for a living. The town characters and amusing events from the author's childhood seem so vaguely familiar, you're likely to think you're reliving your own childhood – or wish you were. *With a Pinch of Sin* is a delightful reminiscence by an author with a startling ability to recall the past. $1.50

A SUMMER BURNING
by Harry J. Boyle

A Canadian farm boy learns the hard facts of life from a young hoodlum fresh out of the slums of Toronto in this piquant novel about a lad's two worlds.

At fifteen, Joey Doyle knew only the world that surrounded the Ontario farm on which he lived – a world of nature and simplicity. But in his sixteenth summer – when Sammy Adams, a tough city boy, came to live at the farm for a few months – Joey was suddenly exposed to a world he had never imagined, in which tobacco and liquor, sex and prostitution, crime . . . and death, played principal roles. $1.50

PaperJacks

MOSTLY IN CLOVER
by Harry J. Boyle

An open door to an era full of warm nostalgia, this is a collection of articles that Harry Boyle contributed to *The Telegram*, edited for book publication, and rescued for a wider immortality than the yellowed newsprint clippings pinned to kitchen walls in rural Ontario. *Harry Boyle* has "a marvellous power to evoke the sounds and sights and smells and feelings of a boyhood gone . . . commands the eye and the heart of the reader in every page". – *Burton T. Richardson in the foreword.* $1.50

HOMEBREW AND PATCHES
by Harry J. Boyle

Crowding around the wood stove with the rest of the family on a bitter January night in the Hungry Thirties brought an indescribable feeling of comfort and security. Full of touching and sometimes hilarious episodes, this book brings to life fiercely fought elections, Valentine's Day box socials and the amazing effects of grandfather's patent medicines. The author has the gift to draw laughter and tears with his memories of growing up in the country. $1.25

PaperJacks

GENTLE PIONEERS
Five Nineteenth-Century Canadians
by Audrey Y. Morris

To the harsh pioneering land of Upper Canada in the 1830s came Susanna Moodie, John W. Dunbar Moodie, Catharine Parr Traill, Thomas Traill and Samuel Strickland. This brilliant biography of a family group shows these people not just as literary and historical personages, but as the individuals they were, with human weaknesses and frailties. It is a vivid portrait of a group who lived through appalling hardships to become noble and "gentle pioneers". $1.50

HONEST ED'S STORY
by Jack Batten

Ed Mirvish, the hero of this 'crazy rags to riches story', isn't just your ordinary multi-millionaire. He got where he is by starting a discount house that would sell nothing but bargains at bargain prices. What made the whole thing take off was Ed's flair for publicity. Ed now owns a theatre (the Royal Alexandra), and his very own street of art galleries and shops. How all this happened – how everything Ed touched turned to gold – is hilariously described in this irreverent success story of Canada's most amazing millionaire. $1.25

PaperJacks

SAVE TAX IN CANADA AND RETIRE AT 45
by Albert Volker

Have you been getting ulcers from the nine-to-five routine? Do you hate turning over thirty percent or more of your pay cheque to the government each year? Do you want to quit the rat race but think you can't afford to? Then read *Save Tax in Canada and Retire at 45*. It tells you how to get money back from the government, and how to use that money to build up a fortune large enough to retire on. This book gives you not just one but ten early retirement plans to choose from. One of them is just right for you. $1.95

HOW YOU CAN MAKE A FORTUNE IN CANADA
by Albert Volker

You can make a fortune ... And you don't have to leave home to do it! Fortunes are now made more easily by Canadians than Americans! In *How You Can Make a Fortune in Canada*, Albert Volker tells you how to do it. He guides you through the maze of insurance gymnastics, and demonstrates the magic of compounding. He suggests ways to keep your dollars out of the government's grasp, and stashed safely away in mutual funds, mortgages, blue-chip stocks. He tells you how to live with inflation and still save money. Mr. Volker tells you how to plan your life style as well as your finances, so that you and your money can live happily ever after. $1.95